Transsex in Societ,

A Sociology of
Male–to–Female
Transsexuals

Frank Lewins

First published 1995 by
MACMILLAN EDUCATION AUSTRALIA PTY LTD
107 Moray Street, South Melbourne 3205

Associated companies and representatives
throughout the world

National Library of Australia
cataloguing in publication data

Lewins, Frank W. (Frank William).
  Transsexualism in society: a sociology of male to female transsexuals.

  Bibliography.
  Includes index.
  ISBN 0 7329 3043 X.
  ISBN 0 7329 3044 8 (pbk.).

  1. Sex change—Social aspects. 2. Transsexuals—Social conditions. I. Title.
305.3

Typeset in Bembo and Frutiger by
Graphic Divine
Printed in Hong Kong
Cover design by Sharon Carr

The author and publishers are grateful to the following for permission to
reproduce copyright material:

Katherine Cummings for the photograph by Reece Scannell on p. 15; Auspac
Media for the Garfield cartoon on p. 140.

Contents

Preface

This study really began when my, then, son announced that he wanted to live as a woman; was attending the Gender Dysphoria Clinic at the Monash Medical Centre in Melbourne; and expected to have gender reassignment surgery after living as a woman for two years, which he would shortly begin! Following successful surgery a few years later, my daughter encouraged me to consider writing a book—a sociological account of transsexualism—to fill a gap. I took that encouragement seriously. I approached the Clinic at the Monash Medical Centre and, with its support, obtained approval from the Centre's ethics committee to interview people who were currently 'on the program' at the Clinic—people known as transsexuals.

I want, first, to thank my daughter, Nicole, her close friends, and other people who agreed to participate in this study. They are the key players in this book and their cooperation, in some cases beyond what one could reasonably expect, has enabled me, hopefully, to say something worthwhile about people who are still the victims of ignorance, prejudice, and discrimination. They are punished for being what they are.

Dr Trudy Kennedy, Coordinator of the Gender Dysphoria Clinic, vigorously supported this project at all times and I owe her a special debt of gratitude. Ms Dawn Wallwork, Clinical Secretary at the Clinic, was effectively an honorary research assistant. Her support, good humour and friendship was indispensable. Also, I must thank Dr Chris Grant, Department of Adult Psychiatry, Monash Medical Centre, and Dr David Clarke, Department of Psychological Medicine, Monash University, who were generous with their time, encouragement and knowledge. They have given this book an added dimension.

At the Australian National University I want to thank Sonya Welykyj in the Department of Sociology for her competent assistance in preparing various parts of the evidence for this book. I also want to thank Michael Flood who, over the past few years, has shown a keen interest in this project and has supplied me with some of the most useful and insightful references I would not otherwise have stumbled across.

Finally, I want to thank the Australian Research Council for funding this project.

F.L.
Canberra
August 1994

1
Introduction

Preamble

Book titles often receive much thought and this one is no exception. I did not want a title that was 'slick' or obtuse. Slick titles can trivialise works that are otherwise important and serious contributions to knowledge. A colleague of mine confirmed this assumption when, somewhat cynically, he suggested I should give this book the title 'A snip here and a snip there and Bob's your aunty'. Given the sensational and trivialising approaches to transsexualism adopted by some sections of the media, where the focus is more on visual images rather than issues, I felt I should give his suggestion a miss. By contrast, obtuse book titles can convey the impression of an anodyne and stuffy treatment of the topic. The result is nobody wants to read the book.

Transsexualism in Society is an attempt to avoid the slick and the obtuse. It is a title chosen to convey two key emphases in this book. First, it focuses on patterns of thinking and behaviour among transsexuals rather than on any individual's characteristics, hence the use of 'transsexualism' rather than 'transsexual'. Second, it examines that thinking and behaviour in its social context by looking at the nature of wider social responses to transsexualism. Those responses are evident in a number of social circles. At the uninformed level, people's understanding ranges from total ignorance of transsexuals to the view that they are sexual deviants. For informed medical professionals, by contrast, a transsexual is not only 'an individual, who is biologically and unambiguously a member of one sex, is convinced, and has been convinced since childhood, that he or she is in fact a member of the opposite sex' (Ross 1986a: 1), but is also a person no longer regarded as a freak or a pervert but someone with a genuine problem 'deserving of compassion, understanding, and appropriate medical and social management' (Walters and Ross 1986: ix). Other professionals view transsexuals as people with an abiding conviction of being in the wrong body, that is, where their preferred gender does not match their biological sex (Money 1988: 53f.).

At a different level, the understanding of transsexuals goes beyond definitions. Although there may be acknowledgement of the important difference between sex and gender, that is, between biological attributes and the socially patterned way of viewing and organising those attributes, there is nevertheless the widespread assumption that there are just two genders and that gender differences are, at least partly if not wholly, dependent on biological sex differences. Arguably, Ross's (1986a) definition of transsexualism above regards sex and gender as the same thing but, in any case, implies a certainty that there are just two genders, as the word 'opposite' suggests.

This book challenges the widespread and taken for granted assumption that there are just two genders and in so doing provides another way of understanding transsexuals. It identifies the significance of the taken for grantedness of that assumption by demonstrating that the act of assuming something to be the case is often more than simply believing certain propositions to be true. It also involves individuals 'knowing' them to be true to the extent that they are never or rarely scrutinised and, least of all, critically analysed. Those sorts of assumptions are 'obviously true'. To adherents, it is as if those assumptions are real or 'out there', where their reality is independent of believers' involvement in originally creating them.[1] In terms of how the wider society understands the notions of sex and gender, as well as transsexuals, there are assumptions of this taken for granted kind. Of course, it needs to be stressed that transsexuals themselves, being a part of that society, share many of those assumptions. As chapter five demonstrates, an important element in the formation of transsexuals' self identity and our understanding of transsexualism is the extent to which those taken for granted assumptions are not equally shared.

One aspect of the taken for granted assumptions surrounding

transsexualism, and one that is not often discussed in the literature, is the uncritical use of the term 'transsexual'. I am not thinking of the use of 'transsexual' by moral entrepreneurs, who uncritically equate the term with sexual deviance. Rather, I am more concerned with use of the term that has the effect of identifying a category of people and, at the same time, explaining their identity and behaviour. To be clear, in medical circles 'transsexualism' is not a diagnosis but, rather, a syndrome or a concurrence of signs and symptoms. As Ross emphasises:

> unfortunately, many who present for treatment ... have diagnosed their symptoms as transsexualism as being the disorder itself, and request gender reassignment surgery as the 'cure' ... we use the term 'transsexualism', in this book, to refer to the presenting symptoms (the belief that one is, or should be, a member of the opposite biological sex), and use 'gender dysphoria' to describe the underlying disorder (1986a: 1).

This careless use of the term 'transsexualism' also exists in wider medical circles and is often compounded by it assuming its own level of reality. Whether it be 'transsexualism' or any other medical term, these notions can become real things that overshadow the people they are applied to. Hence, 'transsexual' or 'the duodenal ulcer in bed ten', for example, can assume a reality or concreteness of their own that is reinforced by their also being seen as 'patients'.

I am not concerned to enter into a lengthy debate about the propriety of the term 'transsexual' but there is a problem of terminology for anyone writing about transsexualism. How do we critically use 'transsexual'? Should we use this term at all? A part of the problem is that it is the only term everyone associated with this area recognises. 'Transgenderist' has been suggested as an alternative but it is unacceptable. Apart from being cumbersome and relatively unknown, it is unsound in terms of the implicit assumptions surrounding its adoption. What it is saying is that if anything undergoes change it is gender and not sex. This study clearly shows that there is good reason to reverse this statement, for it is the sexed body that comes into line with a constant gender or what I would prefer to call psychosexual identity. As will become apparent in chapter two and the last two chapters, gender is still an inadequate concept despite much concern for its rehabilitation. This is not to say that what it refers to—that is, the socially patterned way of viewing and organising sex differences—does not exist. It does, but there is more that the concept has not captured, especially aspects of sexual orientation or desire.

In light of this problem regarding the appropriateness of the term 'transsexual', it is not surprising why many professionals and people viewed as transsexuals are sensitive about misuse of this term but continue to use it. I find myself in the same predicament, especially when it is adopted by biological males who see themselves as 'men' and 'transsexuals' but do not want to live as women and are not contemplating reassignment surgery. Therefore, throughout this book I use 'transsexual' as a term of convenience to identify those people who have made this study possible. On a more methodological note, I am using an operational definition of transsexual. In other words, I am defining transsexual in terms of its concrete manifestation, that is, anyone who has made, or appears to have made, the transition to living permanently in the gender other than the one originally assigned to them.

For the sake of completeness I should also make some comment on the subtitle 'A Sociology of Male to Female Transsexuals'. I deliberately avoid referring to '*the* sociology ...' because I do not pretend to be offering the last word on this topic. There are and will be other studies of transsexuals and transsexualism that lead to other ways of explaining the phenomenon sociologically. Different sociologies of the same phenomenon exist because of variation of key factors, such as the people studied; where they are located; and the competence and vantage point of the sociologist. The issue of vantage point is discussed after a brief comment on the nature of this study.

The Study

The main argument of this book is that, for male to female transsexuals, becoming a woman is a social process with micro and macro dimensions. Micro refers to aspects of social behaviour at the face to face level of interaction, especially where it involves transsexuals' interpretation of sex, gender and the significance of the body. By contrast, the macro dimensions of that process are the wider social patterns and influences in individuals' 'careers'. The extent to which transsexuals pass through some or all of those stages clarifies the nature of the social context in which those individuals are located. Moreover, the extent to which they share the same, or participate in different, social arenas is related to different outcomes of the process of becoming a woman and helps explain some of the difficulties transsexuals face in their transition.

Chapter two provides an important preamble for understanding the macro and micro dimensions of this broad process, which are covered in chapters four and five. It examines our understanding of transsexualism on a number of fronts. It is a selective analysis rather than being a standard and comprehensive review of the literature, for it focuses on the different types of explanatory insights found in biographies of transsexuals, as well as the popular media and clinical, sociological and cross cultural literature. In addition, a number of key works on gender are examined as they are an important precursor to chapters five and six. Finally, chapter six attempts to pull a thread through the main arguments and bring into focus the theoretical and other issues emanating from the study.

The chapter called 'Miranda' is a case study of a transsexual from early childhood to the period following reassignment surgery. Its aim is to present a readable account of the experiences of a *reasonably* typical male to female transsexual and to supplement the selective and somewhat limited picture of transsexualism presented in chapter two.

The focus on male to female transsexuals in this book is solely because of their greater social visibility, cooperation and, hence, accessibility. Of the sixty transsexuals interviewed, only five were female to male. This small proportion did not justify any prominence, nor could they be the basis of any generalisations in this particular study. Clearly, they warrant a separate study to complete the picture.

Almost all interviews were with transsexuals associated with the Gender Dysphoria Clinic at the Monash Medical Centre in Melbourne. Just on 45 per cent of interviewees were interviewed more than twice. Fifteen per cent were interviewed five times or more. Group interviews with six or more transsexuals were conducted on five occasions. In a few cases I lost count of how many interviews I had conducted with a particular person because the interview situation evolved over time into a genuine social contact. A further six transsexuals were interviewed in Canberra and Sydney.[2] As well, a parent of a transsexual spontaneously offered to cooperate in the study and was subsequently interviewed. Other sources of evidence include analysis of files of almost all the post-operative transsexuals held by the Gender Dysphoria Clinic; many discussions with several medical professionals associated with that Clinic; communication with transsexual support groups; and correspondence with five people following feature articles on this research in *The Age* and the *Sydney Morning Herald*.[3]

All interviews with transsexuals were between one and five hours and followed a wide ranging interview guide which covered areas such as: the nature of childhood and adolescence; discovering oneself as a transsexual; education and work history; types of support networks; personal accounts of what it means to be a woman and priorities in becoming a woman; understanding of the notions of sex and gender; the importance of the body; and perceptions of the best and worst aspects of becoming a woman. In the re-interview situation, the most valuable information emerged in the course of spontaneous discussion in which respondents themselves established their own benchmarks and ordering of priorities.

A word of caution is warranted concerning generalising to all transsexuals in Australia. Even though the Gender Dysphoria Clinic draws referrals from all over Australia and neighbouring countries, there is no way of knowing just how representative those referrals are without knowing the number and characteristics of all transsexuals in Australia. It could be the case that transsexuals who are visible by presenting themselves to the Clinic or any medical setting are more confident and self-assured than those who never become a medical 'statistic'. It could also be the case that they were more involved in networks that initially provided information about the existence of the Clinic.

We can, however, be a little more confident in terms of establishing how representative the interviewees in this study were of all transsexuals at the Clinic. Even though there may be an inbuilt bias in that those who cooperated in this study may have particular qualities others lack, such as high self-esteem and cooperativeness, there were some notable similarities and differences. Compared to the two hundred or more post-operative transsexuals who attended the Clinic over the past twenty years, interviewees in this study were more concentrated in or trained for high status, white collar occupations. Nevertheless, most came from or were trained for lower status, manual occupations. This higher proportion of white collar backgrounds among interviewees may be associated with their greater degree of interest in this project. By contrast, interviewees were reasonably representative of the wider category of transsexuals in terms of their birthplace, average age at first visit to the Clinic and average age for reassignment surgery.[4]

Although the transsexuals in this study represent a convenience sample, that sample is large enough for me to be confident of the patterns and processes outlined in the following chapters. Those patterns and processes are an attempt to clarify and explain the process of becoming a woman largely through transsexuals' eyes. However, as 'largely' implies, the identification of key patterns and processes is my attempt to superimpose a sociological frame of reference over transsexuals' experiences.

The Issue of Vantage Point

I, as an author and a sociologist, am also a part of a society in which transsexualism is located. Whether I can critically examine widely held views about sex and gender and stand back from deep seated ethical assumptions about gender reassignment surgery are not straightforward issues. I cannot say how successful I have been in this respect, for that is up to my audience to judge. What all this is referring to is the so-called problem of having a particular vantage point. This issue receives a little more attention than usual because of the nature of my vantage points, that is, as a sociologist and a parent of a transsexual who successfully underwent reassignment surgery several years ago.

Put in the simplest terms, having a vantage point is not in itself the problem. Researchers in all disciplines adopt a number of vantage points. In any particular discipline, scholars hold to shared assumptions about the boundary of their discipline and, therefore, have a particular orientation or theoretical framework when they think about research problems, gather evidence, or write their monographs. Scholars in all scholarly disciplines, for example, start from the vantage point that research is worthwhile. This vantage point is noteworthy for three reasons. First, it is shared by all researchers in all disciplines. Second, it is taken for granted and, therefore, rarely thought about and, finally, because it is not consciously thought about, researchers generally do not realise they are contradicting themselves when they insist they are engaging in value free research. Put differently, researchers claim on the one hand that research should be free of personal evaluations that something is good or bad, desirable or undesirable, yet implicitly hold the view that research is desirable.[5]

If having a vantage point is endemic to research then can it ever be a problem? There are three types of research situation where having a vantage point can be perceived as a problem.

(a) The first involves researchers being unaware of their own vantage points and claiming that their work is 'objective' and the 'truth' concerning a particular topic. The God centred vantage point in medieval medicine and astronomy is often associated with researchers' lack of theoretical development at that time. The problem was that they did not, or could not, recognise that their God centred way of viewing their theories and evidence was just a vantage point. Moreover, they took that God centred view of everything for granted and did not consciously reflect on their own theoretical starting points. Today, we see considerable research being undertaken by women in the area of women's studies, and studies on ethnic categories by migrant researchers. There is nothing unusual about the motivation for that research and there are few problems provided that those researchers recognise their own vantage points.

(b) A different problem arises when researchers fail to declare their vantage point. In this sort of situation, in contrast to the one above, researchers are conscious of their starting point, which is bound up with why they deliberately hide it. Some of the criticisms levelled at research conducted by tobacco companies, for example, include allegations of researchers not only failing to declare their interests or vantage point but also misrepresenting it by telling subjects that their cooperation is being sought in research aimed at improving their health.

(c) The third type of problem arises in the situation in which the researcher's vantage point is criticised because it is perceived as the 'voice' of the subjects under scrutiny.[6] Those who make this criticism claim that researchers have no right to articulate the interests of the subjects they study, such as the poor, women, ethnic categories, and transsexuals, unless they have some entitlement to utter a voice, for example, being 'one of them'. This claim raises the methodological issue surrounding research conducted by 'insiders' and 'outsiders' and no methodologist would deny the problems associated with each approach.[7] These problems are not new and, in response to claims that certain research is inappropriate because it is not conducted from the 'correct' vantage point, really indicate the political rather than methodological aspects of that research. In other words, the view that only certain researchers should be 'allowed' to study certain topics is a view that I enthusiastically reject, largely because it is often a form of the second type of problem discussed above. My firm view is that it is the product of research that should be scrutinised, not the supposed credentials of the researcher.

Put briefly, I do not see any problem in writing about transsexuals from the standpoint of a sociologist and a parent of a transsexual. As a teacher and author in the area of social science methodology, I believe I am aware of most assumptions contained in my own vantage points and I have gone to some lengths to convey them to the readers of this book. I do not accept the view put by some transsexuals that I have 'no right' to be speaking about transsexuals or about women. What I do have to say about transsexuals should stand on its own merits: I am happy to lay it 'on the table'.

Notes

1 This is the process of reification. Berger and Luckmann's (1967) discussion of 'externalization', 'objectivation', and 'internalization' provides a theoretical framework for this process.

2 The source and pre- and post-operative status of male to female transsexuals interviewed are summarised in the table below:

Number of interviews	Location				No.	%
	Gender Dysphoria Clinic		Other			
	post-op	pre-op	post-op	pre-op		
5+	7	1	–	–	8	14.5
2-4	4	12	–	–	16	29.1
1	6	19	4	2	31	55.4
	17	32	4	2	55	100.0

3 Middleton (1993); Mostyn (1993); Crawford (1994).

4

	Interviewees at Clinic	Post-operative cases at Clinic
Average age at first visit to Clinic	31.5 years	30.6 years
Average age for reassignment surgery	32.2 years	33.3 years

Birthplace	Interviewees at Clinic	Post-operative cases at Clinic★	All Australia males only (Australia 1993)
Australia	75.9	74.7	75.2
English-speaking countries	18.5	20.9	9.4
Non-English-speaking countries	5.6	4.4	13.2
Not stated	–	–	2.2
%	100.0	100.0	100.0
No.	49	198	8 362 624

★ Subsequent references to post-operative cases are based on an analysis of the files of 198 individuals. This number represents almost all of a little over two hundred male to female post-operative trans-sexuals who had been associated with the Clinic.

Occupation	Interviewees at Clinic	Post-operative cases at Clinic	All Australia males only (Australia 1993)
Professional, lower professional, managers	33.3	18.9	1.4
Clerical	11.1	4.4	15.0
Service, trades, labourers	55.6	76.7	46.8
Not stated			6.8
%	100.0	100.0	100.0
No.	49	198	8 362 624

Note: In light of changing rates of unemployment over the past two decades, unemployed transsexuals are included based on their occupational backgrounds. The Census figures for all Australian males do not include the unemployed. Given their concentration in the Service/trades/labourer category, if they were added the percentage of Service/trades/labourer for Australian males would be more comparable with the corresponding categories for transsexuals.

Transsexuals in the study population have broad similarities and differences when compared with Tully's (1992: 261-269) sample. I stress 'broad' because Tully breaks his sample up into male to female transsexuals who achieved surgery and those who did not. Also, his occupational categories are different from those used in the table above and he does not provide a comparison with the wider UK workforce. Nevertheless, collapsing both of Tully's sub-categories, both samples presented for the first time at their respective clinics at around the same average age; had similar high proportions who were or had been married; and had similar proportions who had children. The samples differ in that Tully's seemed to have a more even spread of occupations, with a lower proportion of professionals and unskilled. Also, his subjects had a far higher incidence of previous criminal activity.

5 The discussion of vantage points in research is related to the notion of theory dependence or theory ladenness, which is dealt with at length in Lewins (1992a).

6 The concept of 'voice' owes considerable debt to Hirschman (1970). Although I am not applying the concept to people in firms and organisations, I am using it in Hirschman's wider sense, that is,

as any attempt at all to change ... an objectionable state of affairs ... through various types of actions and protests, including those that are meant to mobilize public opinion ... voice is nothing but a basic portion and function of any political system, known sometimes also as 'interest articulation' (1970: 30).

7 See Lewins (1992a; 1992b) for a preliminary discussion of the issues surrounding research conducted by 'insiders' and 'outsiders'.

2
What Do We Know About Transsexualism?

Asking what we know about transsexualism implicitly poses the obverse question, that is—'what is it that we don't know?' This chapter addresses both questions by selectively looking at a wide range of approaches that go beyond the clinical and socio-cultural categories used by Bolin (1987a) to include autobiographies and the print and electronic media. My aims are to show how each approach has its own style and type of question it seeks to answer and to identify the answered and unanswered questions posed about transsexualism. I am less concerned about what each researcher or author says. Therefore, the analysis of these approaches, especially the clinical and socio-cultural, is selective. In any case, a comprehensive review of the various literatures would not only be very lengthy but also repetitious of what already exists elsewhere.[1]

Autobiographies

What do transsexuals' autobiographies tell us about transsexualism? Contrary to the frequently heard comment among transsexuals that 'once you've read one you've read them all', they do contain revealing themes. At a purely descriptive level, autobiographies contain similar 'case histories'. Notwithstanding the reasonable comment that autobiographies are often written shortly after reassignment surgery, when transsexuals are 'still wrapped in the euphoria of the newly acquired physical body' (Ratnam, Goh, and Tsoi 1991: iv), they are similar not only in content but also in terms of the areas in which authors place personal significance. The key areas are:

(a) the long personal history of tension between biological sex and preferred gender or, as many transsexuals put it, having a conviction of being in the wrong body. Katherine Cummings, a well-known transsexual, who is pictured opposite, eloquently captures this tension:

> I can only reiterate the image so often used by transsexuals, that of feeling locked inside a body in which they do not belong, looking through the eyes of that body as they might through the eyeholes of a mask, or from the windows of a cell. The latter image is probably more appropriate, for masks are usually adopted voluntarily, to enhance power, mystery or beauty. In the case of a transsexual locked inside a prison of flesh and blood there is a constant ache for emancipation and sense of wonder that no one senses the cries for help from the prisoner within (1992: 209);

(b) the awareness and experience of being different as a child, often accompanied by bullying and teasing at school;

(c) the psychological struggle to reconcile the conflict between what the mind is demanding and what the body every day seems to be saying. Jan Morris describes her own conflict in terms of 'living a falsehood'. She adds:

> I was in masquerade, my female reality, which I had no words to define, clothed in a male pretence ... I felt that in wishing so fervently, and so ceaselessly, to be transplanted into a girl's body, I was aiming only at a more divine condition, an inner reconciliation (1987: 18);

(d) and the negative social responses to a life of overt transsexualism.

Although almost all autobiographies are written by male to female transsexuals,[2] these emphases also appear in the autobiographical sentiments of female to male transsexuals, such as the relatively well-known autobiography by Peter Stirling (1989). These themes are only mentioned at this point for they assume

Katherine Cummings

more prominence in the next chapter, which looks at the personal case history of Miranda, and especially in chapter four, which deals with the macro aspects of the process of becoming a woman.

At another level transsexuals' autobiographies reveal a more implicit theme. In each case the author's personal history is the method of clarifying transsexualism, but only the author's transsexualism. Tully touches on this point concerning auto- biographies when he says that

> these stories and apologias have been put together with the overriding purposes of justifying the transsexual status. Events and thoughts are marshalled together to demonstrate, to con- vince. They are a form of rhetoric ... (1992: xiv-xv).

However, it is more than justification. Transsexual authors, by choosing the autobiographical approach, look from the present to the past and, through their historical narrative, attempt to link them. Now the obvious retort to this comment is what else could be expected of an autobiography? Is it not, by definition, a per- sonal history? True, but the key question here is not 'what is an autobiography?' but 'why is it that transsexuals who decide to go into print choose their own autobiography to provide insight into transsexualism?' It is not as if there are no other alternatives. They could write a novel,[3] an account of their current life from a new perspective, or something that linked the present with the future. Alternatively, given the literary talents of some transsexuals, such as Jan Morris (1987) and Katherine Cummings (1992), they could write a research monograph.

Transsexuals' choice of autobiography provides additional insight into transsexualism because not only does it provide the opportunity to construct the self by making sense of the past, but also it illustrates the need to account for or explain the present. Focus on the passage from the past to the present, especially in light of the four key areas described above, strongly suggests a developmental or processual understanding and raises the ques- tion of whether all transsexuals see their transsexualism the same way. To be clear, by 'processual' I am thinking of an individual's overt transsexualism as a process within a social context rather than a quality, such as something like hair colour that is deter- mined by a genetic factor. This is not necessarily to deny genetic causes but to identify in transsexuals' own understanding of their situation the sorts of questions social scientists need to explore. As the following chapters indicate, this book places great significance on the processual nature of transsexualism. As the section on clin- ical literature points out, however, social process does not necessarily negate genetic causes of transsexualism.

Mention of causes of transsexualism provides the link with another more implicit insight into transsexuals' autobiographies. Just as we gain from identifying what is implicitly present, we can also gain from establishing the 'silences' or those areas which authors overlook or choose not to stress. There are two silences that are salient for the sociological approach of this book. The first is that the search for causes of transsexualism is not a priority. This silence is the obverse of the personal, historical narrative outlined above. The more the personal domain assumes priority, the more unimportant is the *explanation* of transsexualism in society. Also, this silence, by implicitly stressing authors' concern for the personal dimensions of their own transsexuality, raises a question about the level of personal confidence required to write a book about oneself. Katherine Cummings goes so far as to admit to 'a strong element of narcissism in both transvestism and transsexualism' (1992: 18) and, in quoting the words of the Abbe de Choisy (1644–1724), notes that 'we always love ourselves more than we love others' (1992: 19). The silence surrounding the search for the causes of transsexualism thus leads to the question 'Are transsexuals who write autobiographies among the most narcissistic and self-confident of their number, or is narcissism a recurring quality among all transsexuals?' This question is important not so much for its answer but, rather, because it suggests caution in assuming autobiographies are written by 'typical' transsexuals.

The second silence in transsexuals' autobiographies is any stress on the causal link between transsexualism and physical sex, especially the seeking of gender reassignment surgery to enable one to have a sex life that accords with previously frustrated sexual desires. This link, which will be touched on below, is the sort of association drawn in the print media and one which many transsexuals find difficult to understand. It is acknowledged in autobiographies in a variety of ways. For instance, in her dismissive approach to the significance of sexual activity in her earlier life, Jan Morris indicates the nature of its silence in *Conundrum*:

One of the genuine and recurrent surprises of my life concerns the importance to men of physical sex. I was baffled by it when I left my poor friend distraught and apprehensive at the door of the Trieste brothel, when he would have had a far happier

time, I felt sure, going to the pictures ... And even now, so
many years older and more experienced, I am taken aback by
the intensity with which mature, kind and cultured men,
reading earlier drafts of this book, looked in it for revelations
about the sexual act (1987: 55).

Katherine Cummings is equally clear, although more direct and
personal:

my life is as celibate since my operation as it was immediately
before. My transsexualism is, and always was, inside my head,
not my loins. There is room for only one love in my life and
she is lost to me (1992: 226).

In short, transsexuals' autobiographies help identify questions
we need to ask, such as whether patterns in transsexuals' histories
point to transsexualism being a process rather than a quality;
whether the transsexuals who have written autobiographies are
even reasonably representative of a wider category of transsexuals,
especially as it appears transsexuals in general 'ache for quiet
"undercover" lives' (Tully 1992: xiv);[4] and whether there is any
relationship between transsexualism and what we might loosely
call sexual orientation and the desire for physical sex.

The Print and Electronic Media

This section is considerably briefer than that above simply
because the print and, especially, the electronic media have not
shed much light on transsexualism. This observation is not confined to Australia, for Ratnam, Goh, and Tsoi (1991: iii),
members of an internationally known team that works with
transsexuals in Singapore, believe that the media 'have aroused
more confusion than empathy' on this topic. In Britain, King's
(1993: 96-132) more detailed analysis of the coverage of transvestism and transsexualism in newspapers and magazines from the
period 1950 to 1983, supplemented by a small number of radio

and television items, clearly reveals more about the nature of the British media than transsexualism.

The failure of the media in Australia to increase our understanding of transsexualism is in spite of the large number of articles that have appeared in newspapers and popular magazines in recent years. Magazine stories, especially those targeted at women, are the least informative and are written to a predictable recipe. Generally they are brief; contain a photograph of the transsexual, sometimes photographs 'before and after' transition; they describe the transsexual's history, emphasising personal 'torment'; they mention, but do not discuss, issues such as legal rights and changing birth certificates; and often adopt startling titles such as 'Tragedy of the mum who became a man'.[5] These articles do not raise any serious questions, let alone address them, and are what Katherine Cummings calls ' "Gee-whiz" stories' (1992: 206) designed to entertain and titillate.

By contrast, newspapers contain two distinct approaches to transsexualism, which are largely a function of the particular newspaper they appear in. Alongside the same 'Gee-whiz stories' characteristic of popular magazines, typified by headlines such as 'Sex-changer ditched by her dream lover!' (*Truth* 1990) and 'Ring-in Delores stuns glamor judges' (*Daily Sun* 1985), there are serious feature articles and news stories. The latter have largely concentrated on legal issues, for example, the role of biological sex and transsexuals' right to marry, entitlements to government benefits and protection under anti-discrimination legislation. Some of the feature articles in recent years, especially in *The Age* (for example, Lopez 1991; Middleton 1993; Crawford 1994) and the *Sydney Morning Herald* (for example, Bell 1989; Mostyn 1993), have attempted to come to grips with sensitive issues such as those concerning family ties and the law.

The electronic media also have a patchy record in contributing to our understanding of transsexualism. Radio National presented a series on the progress and views of a transsexual in 'The Health Report', which ran from August 1987 to December 1989. It was written and presented by Katherine Cummings, who believes it was a 'worthwhile project' (Cummings 1992: 198). ABC television did not fare so well when in 1989 Peter Couchman devoted one of his programs to transsexualism. The title of the program 'Wedding Belles' gives some idea of what attracts much television to this sort of topic. Couchman's questions indicated he was inadequately informed on key legal and human rights issues facing transsexuals, which he largely avoided. Instead he pursued questions about transsexuals' sexuality and sexual capacity. The only informative dimension in the program was the nature of the responses from the audience of informed professionals and transsexuals, who repeatedly attempted to move the line of questioning to a different agenda (see also Cummings 1992: 203-205).

For the sake of completeness, I must mention the '60 Minutes' story on transsexualism presented by the television journalist Richard Carleton. I imagine many transsexuals were deeply depressed after seeing that program, for it added little to our understanding of the topic and it also succeeded in trivialising the issues. Notable was Richard Carleton's interview with two transsexuals. Indicative of his shallow approach, he concluded the interview by asking them whether, in light of their different genders, they might consider 'getting together'!

Finally, I will add my own experience, which is consistent with television's approach to transsexualism. Following the feature stories in *The Age* (Middleton 1992) and the *Sydney Morning Herald* (Mostyn 1992) on my research on transsexualism, a commercial television channel wanted to interview me on a well-known current affairs program. The only condition, which was not negotiable, was that my 'transsexual daughter' also appear on the program. I refused the interview.

Two important questions are implicit in the manner in which the print and electronic media have handled the phenomenon of transsexualism. The first, especially in light of transsexuals' reactions to media accounts, is the same question that emerged from autobiographies, that is, is there any relationship between transsexualism and sexual orientation and the desire for physical sex? The second question concerns the media bias towards accounts of male to female transsexuals. Is it, for example, a result of their greater incidence or is it related to the alleged lower tolerance of males cross dressing and sex changing? The evidence, as King (1993: 106-107) notes, poses problems for both these explanations.

There is, finally, the question of the role of the media. Does the media's coverage of transsexualism have any social consequences? This question deserves brief consideration given the claims made by commentators, such as Raymond (1979), Billings and Urban (1982) and Sagarin (1978). They suggest that media coverage of transsexualism, principally, reproduces current medical thinking; legitimates in the public's eyes the phenomenon of transsexualism; and supports the so-called dominant order (King 1993: 96-132). Like many studies of the role of the media, these claims are strong on profound, macro claims but are weak when it comes to evidence to support them. In Australia, at least, the medical profession does not have a unified response to transsexualism and reassignment surgery. So which particular aspect of medical thinking is the media reproducing? Notwithstanding the last point and barring a few exceptions, the media's sensationalising and trivialising of transsexualism certainly bears no relationship to the thinking of medical professionals associated with transsexuals. As to media support of the dominant order, this claim is similar to those claims beyond the limits of evidence made about the dominant ideology, which has received considerable critical attention (see Abercrombie *et al.* 1980).

Clinical Research

The substantial clinical literature[6] on transsexualism has grown along with its increasing social visibility and claims that transsexuals 'are no longer regarded as freaks or perverts but as people with genuine problems deserving of compassion, understanding, and appropriate medical and social management' (Walters and Ross 1986: ix). These claims are made by some medical professionals alongside other colleagues' considerable doubt about the desirability of facilitating gender transition, especially with gender reassignment surgery (Collyer 1994; Goh 1991: 1, 15, 21; Bolin 1987a: 46-47). The wide ranging clinical literature on transsexualism contains two themes that are relevant to this study. The first is the absence of any serious consideration of the role of social factors in examining the aetiology of transsexualism. Second, there is the nature of the vantage point of the clinical observer, who starts from the assumption that transsexualism is, medically, an abnormal state.

Social factors associated with transsexualism are often only mentioned rather than discussed in detail (for example, Snaith *et al.* 1993). They include claims that transsexualism has a long history (Green 1969, 1974; Ross 1986a; Goh 1991: 2)[7] and that it exists in all societies and ethnic categories (Green 1974: 3-13; *Lancet* 1991: 603), although its prevalence varies in western countries (Ross 1986b: 19). We also see that transsexuals are more prevalent in rigid gender role societies and in low income social categories.[8] Consequently, they have lower levels of education, are not concentrated in high status occupations and have high levels of unemployment.[9] Generally, they are not feminists, especially those who are male to female, and are 'often relatively asexual'.[10] Also frequently mentioned is the association between transsexualism and positive relations with the mother and somewhat negative relations with the father, characterised by absence, lack of interest and/or remoteness.[11] By contrast, more isolated social correlates of transsexualism include claims that Catholics are over-represented in samples of transsexuals, whose parents are more religious and homophobic than the rest of the population.[12]

These patterns and correlates are often implicated in discussions of the aetiology of transsexualism, which is still imprecisely understood and would appear, at minimum, to entail an array of different types of causal factors.[13] This point about multi-causality warrants some elaboration because it seems fairly definite that, within the clinical approach, transsexualism cannot be wholly explained by either a 'nature' or 'nurture' theory (Goh 1991: 15-19). For the purposes of this chapter, it is not necessary to sub-divide the nurture approach in the way Docter (1988) does,[14] but rather to make clear that it includes both the alleged psychological causal factors and the broader sociological factors that most clinical commentators (for example, Goh 1991) play down. A strengthening of the multi-causal nature of transsexualism is evident from a critical examination of some of the assumptions embedded in the nurture case.

A good place to begin this examination is the research on intersexed infants, that is, where a child's assigned sex contradicts some aspect of sex determination, such as chromosomes, gonads, genitals or hormones. This research is said to demonstrate a

consistent environmental input, pointing in the direction of
being a boy or a girl, to overrule the biological contribution to
sexual identity (Green 1974: 25).

It is worth looking at the nature of the argument in this research
because it is 'most commonly quoted to explain the development
of gender identity' (Goh 1991: 16). John Money and Patricia
Tucker's case histories of intersexed individuals are revealing and
it is useful to quote from one at length to convey the particular
individual's depth of conviction about his sexual identity:

> there was the man who first came to Johns Hopkins when he
> was twenty-four years old. Even with his medical history open
> on the desk, it is hard for the experienced medical professionals
> who have followed his case to believe that he was ever anything
> but a normal male. Nothing in his appearance, manner, ges-
> tures, or conversation betrays the fact that genetically and
> gonadally he was born female. He had looked like a boy at
> birth, although there were no testicles and the penis was some-
> what deformed. He was labelled male and raised as a boy on
> the assumption that the testicles were there but had not
> descended ... it never occurred to him to doubt that he was a
> boy who would become a man and marry a woman. By the
> age of seven he had singled out a little girl as his sweetheart. As
> he approached puberty, his breasts started to develop and his
> body began to round out. Those who believe that anatomy is
> destiny would expect these anatomical developments to be
> reflected in his outlook. On the contrary, he regarded his
> breasts as a deformity and wanted only one thing from the
> medical profession—to be rid of them. An exploratory opera-
> tion at that time revealed ovaries, a uterus and a vagina that
> opened internally into the urethra near the neck of the bladder,
> but no male reproductive system. Even when the boy under-
> stood, as he described it, that 'they'd found some kind of
> female apparatus in there by mistake' and that he would never
> be able to sire offspring, his concept of himself as a male
> remained unshaken; it never seemed to him that he might

'really' be a girl. The female organs were removed, eliminating the menstrual process which had just begun, and he was put on replacement male hormones to stop breast development, distribute his body fat in a masculine pattern, and direct masculine bone growth. His voice soon began to deepen and his beard to grow. At nineteen this man had a passionate love affair with a girl, and the following year he met and fell in love with the girl he later married ... Two years after their wedding he reported with dreamy sincerity, 'We think we're the luckiest people in the world' (1977: 49-50).

Money and Tucker's assumption is that gender identity develops 'independently of, and in contrast to, the individual's chromosome or gene complement, his gonads, internal and external genitals and secondary sexual characteristics, singly or in combination' (Goh 1991: 16). The argument holds that the gender identity of rearing is imprinted very early, being well established by two to three years of age. The type of case above is used to demonstrate the claim that, in spite of an individual's biological sex and attempts by others to change his/her gender identity, that identity will continue to correspond to the gender of rearing.

Turning this approach to transsexualism, one needs to be able to explain why males reared as 'boys' do not grow into 'men', especially in rigid gender role societies. The claim of this 'assignment theory' is that transsexualism is the result of 'either conscious or unconscious rearing of the child in opposition to his or her anatomical gender' (Goh 1991: 17). Mention of 'unconscious' poses a problem because this explanation can be used as an *ad hoc* modification so that there can be no exceptions to the rule. In other words, despite clear evidence plainly pointing to a child being reared unambiguously as a boy or girl, the presence of transsexualism only demonstrates that that child was unconsciously reared in the other gender. The arbiter of this sort of claim should be evidence and not the dogmatic convictions of the proponent.

The singular causal assumption in 'assignment theory' is challenged by another nurture approach. Stressing the significance of events in infancy, Stoller's (1968: 108-125) psychoanalytic theory places causal significance on the mother's contribution to boyhood transsexualism. The nature of the 'symbiotic fusion' with the mother leads to altered personality development, resulting in a 'feminine core identity' (Docter 1988: 66–68). As Stoller (1968: 264) himself put it, transsexualism results from 'too much mother made possible by too little father'.

It is, however, research on the role of neonatal hormones within the nature approach that poses a greater challenge to the exclusive role of any nurture theory. According to Goh (1991: 17), the 'psychoneuroendocrine theory is by far the most well-studied hypothesis', which holds that brain exposure to an abnormal concentration of sex hormones during fetal and early postnatal life is a major determinant of gender confusion and, subsequently, transsexualism. This theory, which has a precursor in the work of Benjamin (1966), is frequently used to counter the 'assignment theory' proposed by John Money, especially by invoking the well-known research on gender reversal among male pseudo-hermaphrodites in the Dominican Republic. This research argues that an enzyme deficiency among those males means that male sex hormones, although present, are not effective in producing normal external genitalia. They are reported to be raised unambiguously as females from birth but at puberty, when the testes become functional, secondary sexual characteristics, such as deepening of the voice and penile growth, occur. Those males then revert to a male identity and orientation thus demonstrating that hormonal influence rather than patterns of rearing is the most significant factor in shaping the differentiation of male identity. Widespread doubt exists, however, as to whether those males are raised unambiguously as females. It is suggested that there is a cultural awareness among parents and children of the known careers of such children and, hence, there is an expectation of, and even anticipatory socialisation towards, later adoption of male gender identity (Goh 1991: 18–19).[15]

This brief excursion into the aetiology of transsexualism clearly demonstrates a number of points. It suggests the inadequacy of any one factor to account for transsexualism. At the same time, acknowledgement that nurture-type explanations have some role in the aetiology of transsexualism suggests that transsexualism is a process rather than a quality. Also, given the focus of some sections of the media on the relationship between transsexualism, especially reassignment surgery, and transsexuals' desire for and legitimation of physical sexual activity, it is notable that there is a silence in the clinical literature on this topic. In fact, the Singapore specialists explicitly and forcefully play down this connection, arguing that 'acquiring an identity from surgical procedures is of greater importance than acquiring functioning genitalia for the purpose of sex' (Ratnam, Goh, Anandakumar, and Tham 1991: 57).

A closer look at the second theme—that is, clinicians' uncritical assumption that transsexualism is an abnormal state[16] —involves more than noting transsexuals being regarded as 'patients', their 'treatment' in the form of 'psychotherapeutic intervention' (Edelmann 1986), and listing transsexualism as a psychiatric condition in the American Psychiatric Association's *Diagnostic and Statistical Manual* (Docter 1988: 25-26; see also Tully 1992: 5-6). An implicit assumption in the clinical literature is that there is some normal standard alongside which transsexualism can be judged as abnormal and, therefore, in need of treatment. It is not the visible variety of psychosexual identities that prompts scrutiny in terms of its aetiology but a particular facet seen to be pathological. Given that everything has a cause(s), even heterosexuality, it is not only clinicians' focus on aetiology that is worth noting but also the significance they attribute to the thing caused, that is, transsexualism. I have not come across any clinical literature that questions its own assumptions and scrutinises its vantage point.

The language of professionals in clinical settings illustrates the assumption that transsexualism is pathological. Transsexualism is regarded, for example, as 'a symptom of an underlying *disturbance* of gender identity, [i.e.] gender dysphoria' (Walters 1988: 22, emphasis added) and 'the more extreme degree of the *disorder*' (*Lancet* 1991: 603, emphasis added; see also Goh 1991: 5). The reality of a 'disorder' is reinforced by a standard clinical concern for its prevalence in a given society and the need for treatment. This taken for granted assumption of pathology sits uneasily beside wide discrepancies in estimates of prevalence,[17] the unknown aetiology of transsexualism, and the lack of any satisfactory explanation in the so-called diagnosis of 'primary gender dysphoria'.[18] This term is saying little more than that the reason transsexualism is manifest is because those transsexuals have a life long, intense confusion about their gender.

The Socio-cultural Approach

The socio-cultural approach to transsexualism is diverse and includes actual research on transsexualism, cross cultural studies and the wider and burgeoning literature on sex and gender. It attempts to explain transsexualism by analysing it in its social context, that is, by asking how the nature of that context, such as wider conceptions and practice surrounding sex and gender, affect the appearance of transsexualism. Whereas the clinical approach adopts an 'internal' focus, concentrating on the individual and searching for biological and psychological factors that do not go beyond the family, the socio-cultural approach analyses the role of 'external' factors 'in the extant socio-cultural system' (Bolin 1987a: 59). A strong, general theme in the socio-cultural approach is that transsexualism is closely linked to the social organisation of gender roles and relations and that, contrary to widespread taken for granted assumptions about the givenness of those gender roles, they are socially constructed and, therefore, mutable. However, more noteworthy are the varying sub-themes that are dealt with below.

It is not appropriate for this study to consider the socio-cultural literature as 'roughly divided' into the sociological and anthropological (Bolin 1987a: 47), where the former is constituted by the contributions of the ethnomethodologists and the latter by cross cultural research on gender variation. Although these contributions provide worthwhile insights, they have in recent years been supplemented by specific sociological studies of a non-ethnomethodological kind and insights from the wider academic scrutiny of the notions of sex and gender. Given the accessibility of that earlier socio-cultural literature, I will refer to the main contributions in passing and concentrate more on recent literature in explicating three identifiable sub-themes. Although they overlap it is worthwhile analysing each in turn.

Doing gender

Starting with the more micro level insights, the first sub-theme derives from ethnomethodological studies and revolves around the idea that gender is a property of individuals that is attained and constantly maintained. Contrary to widespread taken for granted assumptions that it is a natural, static quality based on an individual's genitalia, we are, as Kessler and McKenna put it, involved in an 'ongoing process of "doing" gender in everyday interactions' (1985: 126). Their understanding of gender is similar to that of Garfinkel and Stoller (1967), Kando (1973), and Feinbloom (1976) and focuses on how male to female transsexuals in everyday situations maintain their own identity as 'women' and attempt to ensure that others 'attribute' the appropriate gender to them. Given the 'natural attitude' towards gender—that is, that the wider public take for granted that there are only two genders that are natural and immutable—people known to be 'transsexuals' represent a violation of this assumption. Therefore, by presenting themselves as 'women' and not something in between, transsexuals reinforce a taken for granted, dichotomous view of gender. This point is picked up by Bolin (1987a: 51) when discussing Kessler and McKenna's *Gender: An Ethnomethodological Approach*. She notes the existence of

culturally constituted 'natural attitudes' about gender revealed by transsexuals who, through their violation of these attitudes, paradoxically support American cultural beliefs about gender: There are only two genders that are fixed and cannot be changed or transferred, genitals are primarily insignias of gender, exceptions to the dual gender system 'are not to be taken seriously', one is either a male or a female (not in between), and the dichotomization of gender into males and females is natural ... transsexualism is itself a symptom of this dual gender classification. In this regard, Kessler and McKenna state: 'In a society that could tolerate lack of correspondence (between gender and genitalia), there would be no transsexual individuals. There would be men with vaginas and women with penises or perhaps different signs of gender'.[19]

At present, though, there appears to be no society that tolerates routine lack of correspondence between gender and genitalia. Alongside Bolin's and Kessler and McKenna's claim, however, that 'genitals are primarily insignias of gender', it needs to be stressed that the genitals are not the *primary* insignias of gender in everyday life. It is, instead, outward, morphological *appearance* that enables us to attribute gender but, given the natural attitude to gender, we rarely think how we use appearance in that attribution process. Woodhouse brings out this point in her study of transvestites:

> the appearance of femininity denotes female sex and the appearance of masculinity, male sex. This assumption is so deeply ingrained and so completely taken for granted that in the course of our everyday lives we rarely, if ever, think about it. It just does not occur to us that we do not know the sex of most people and that all we have to go on is appearance (1989: 3).

To illustrate the nature of the taken for grantedness of gender in society, it is worth picking up on Bolin's claim that 'no one in our culture is immune from the pervasiveness of social definitions of gender, including scientists involved in gender research' (1987a: 50-51). As a social scientist writing about her research among male transvestites, Woodhouse captures the profound significance of the taken for grantedness of gender in relating her own experience. It is worth quoting her at length:

> After my first visit I began to think about the way I saw cross-dressed men. Did I treat them as men, or as women, or as men-appearing-as-women? This was highlighted by an incident which occurred during my third visit to TV/TS. While chatting with a transvestite I had met previously, I noticed someone standing at the counter. She looked different from the others present, dressed in a quiet manner with light make-up and glasses. Her own hair was done in an ordinary, unelaborate style. Unremarkable in appearance, she could have been a secretary or receptionist. Not having met her before, I wanted to introduce myself and, hopefully, find out more about her. But I found myself unable to approach her until I knew 'what' she was. In other words, I realised that my social manner towards her would be determined by my knowledge of her sexual

status. The everyday, taken for granted assumption that gender appearance indicates biological sex broke down in this setting and thus the fragility of that commonplace expectation was thrown into sharp relief. She could have been a transvestite or, indeed, she could have been a real woman. *I* was unable to tell. The very fact that I had to ascertain her biological status from someone else before approaching her underlined the ways in which social interaction is firmly based on the unconscious expectations we use to identify people and place them in stereotyped categories (1989: 29-30, her emphasis).

This point foreshadows an important question that will be considered later. Do transsexuals learn how to read the public's 'natural attitude' towards gender so that they are more able to construct and manipulate their appearance when 'doing gender' in everyday life?

The social construction of gender

The strongest sub-theme running through the socio-cultural literature is the view that gender is socially constructed or, in other words, is dependent on its social context rather than being a pre-determined category inextricably linked to biological sex differences. This theme is found in all facets of the socio-cultural approach, that is, ethnomethodological and cross cultural studies, recent research on transsexualism, and the wider literature focusing on sex and gender. It is not my intention to embark on a lengthy literature review but, instead, I want selectively to draw on that literature to identify variation in the way gender is categorised and linked to biological sex differences and sexual orientations. I also want to show the implications of that variation for understanding transsexualism.

To grasp the significance of the social constructionist approach in relation to transsexualism, it is worth identifying the ways in which scholars have viewed the relationship between sex and gender. The following possibilities warrant some elaboration:

1 only 'sex' differences exist; there is no 'gender'
2 'sex' and 'gender' are the same thing
3 'sex' determines 'gender'
4 'sex' and 'gender' are 'additive' (see below)

5 'gender' is the only important concept; 'sex' differences are
irrelevant

6 'gender' determines 'sex'.

In practice, not all these relationships are equally important, for
the first two are so much a part of our everyday experience and
recent history that they do not require lengthy comment. The
first, for example, merely indicates that before the concept of
gender was articulated (see Money 1988: 52-53),[20] biological sex
differences were understood as sufficient for the explanation of
human differentiation in the social realm. Concerning the
second, sex and gender are often used interchangeably at an
everyday level, which is a confusion that spills over into the
scholarly realm (Kessler and McKenna 1985: 7).

The view that sex determines gender has been the dominant
assumption by far in the academic literature. Kessler and
McKenna (1985: viii) put this position strongly when they say
that 'it has been generally taken for granted that *fundamentally*
gender is a consequence of a biological blueprint' (their emphasis). Connell (1987: 67) puts the central assumption more directly,
that is, 'society registers what nature decrees'. He cites books,
such as Desmond Morris's *The Naked Ape* and Lionel Tiger's *Men
in Groups*, as the more obvious examples of a 'pseudo-biological'
approach that does not 'rest on serious biological investigation of
human social life' but, rather, on 'a series of loose analogies'
(1987: 68). This biological reductionist stance could be summarised by Morris's words from *The Naked Ape*, which Connell
quotes:

> it is the biological nature of the beast that has moulded the
> social structure of civilisation, rather than the other way around
> (1987: 68).

A less obvious example of this 'natural difference' approach to
sex and gender is the notion that society and nature are additive.
Additive means that natural differences between males and
females are insufficient to account for the complexity of social
differentiation. 'Society therefore *culturally elaborates* the distinction between the sexes' by stressing, for instance, the

distinctiveness of men's and women's clothing which emphasises their distinctive bodies (Connell 1987: 73, his emphasis). Germaine Greer's views on transsexualism are a good example of this additive approach. Although critical of the way femaleness has become overlain and confused with certain notions of femininity, her denial of the validity of the gender of male to female transsexuals rests on an essentialist assumption that there is something immutable about being a man, that is, his original biology. Her own words best convey this premise. In her review of Jan Morris's *Conundrum*, which originally appeared in the *Evening Standard* in 1974, she notes that

> Jan Morris is a man who has eaten a great many pills, artificial hormones and the crystallized essence of the urine of pregnant mares, a man who has had his penis cut off, but a man nevertheless (1986: 189).

Some years later the same position is evident again. Writing about a male to female transsexual whose behaviour seems to have got under her skin, Greer cynically remarks that

> we might not be surprised to find bureaucrats accepting the idea that the female is no more than a castrated male, in flat contradiction of the biology that tells us that maleness is no more than damage to one chromosome of the female set ... If you want to be female so badly that you are prepared to mutilate yourself, and if the doctor who mutilated you will write you a letter saying that the change is permanent, then the beneficent state will declare that you are what you are not, a woman ... [M]y argument ... is that the genuine difference has been obscured by a series of phoney differences. Femaleness has been distorted into femininity; womanhood has become permanent girlishness ... Gender transience is a lie (1989).

On the one hand, Greer wants to demonstrate the contingent nature of rigid gender stereotyping to show that it can be changed yet, on the other hand, contradicts herself by denying transsexuals' gender shift in becoming women. Woodhouse (1989: 80) correctly notes, she 'cannot have it both ways'.

Connell (1987: 74-75), in criticising this additive conception of sex and gender, notes that the social is often emphasised to the point of not giving any significance to the empirical reality of certain biological events in our lives, that is, events concerning the body such as pleasure, pain, body contact and so on.[21] This criticism could also be applied to early second wave feminists, who, as Connell (1987: 67) notes, 'implied that all sex differences are socially produced'. In other words, gender rather than sex differences is the important means of differentiation in explaining the place of women in society.

On the intellectual front, the assumption that gender differences are somehow the result of biological sex differences has been largely discredited by a substantial body of literature. There is a growing tide of academic opinion that supports the idea that gender is constructed in a social context and can even be chosen instead of gender dichotomy being 'forced upon us by nature' (Connell 1987: 75). Here the role of biological sex differences is turned on its head. Rather than determining gender, they are determined by it. This is well put by Kessler and McKenna:

> Scientists construct dimorphism where there is continuity. Hormones, behavior, physical characteristics, developmental processes, chromosomes, psychological qualities have all been fitted into gender dichotomous categories ... Biological, psychological, and social differences do not lead to our seeing two genders. Our seeing two genders leads to the 'discovery' of biological, psychological, and social differences (1985: 163).

Connell makes a similar point when referring to the 'mirror structure', that is, something that reflects 'familiar social arrangements', such as gender dichotomy, as if 'required by nature' (1987: 72-73; see also Bolin 1987a: 51).

The social construction of gender is corroborated by the principal insights of anthropologists who have scrutinised gender from a cross cultural perspective. Possibly the most well-known research of this kind has been that on the berdache, a social category among North American natives. As males, the berdache adopt the female gender role, which Kessler and McKenna (1985: 29) view as a 'third gender category, separate from male and female', arguing that this is evidence of the contingent nature of western gender dichotomies. Bolin (1987a: 53–54), however, points out that the western categories of 'homosexual', 'transvestite' and 'transsexual' have been employed to account for the berdache in different circumstances. Despite warnings though about the need for precision of terms, inconsistency and confusion continue, especially where the berdache might be viewed as transsexuals. This is because the berdache are associated with a particular form of behaviour and not 'identity or personal motivation, central attributes in the definition of Western transsexualism' (Bolin 1987a: 54). Despite possible caveats in the case of the berdache, cross cultural research on gender reveals ways of attributing gender other than biological sex differences and the non-universality of two genders. In terms of transsexualism, this literature helps challenge the taken for granted link of sex and gender and raises the question as to whether they are related at all.[22] Moreover, cross cultural insights seriously challenge the assumption thematic in the clinical approach that transsexualism is pathology. This point is more forcefully put by Grimm:

> the mere existence of living examples of alternate gender statuses in other cultures would seem to fly in the face of psychiatric interpretations of transsexualism. The general acceptance in other cultures and, especially, cases of high status granted to individuals who cross gender lines, suggest that we should look at the importance of the social construction of reality instead of assuming pathological roots to the variant behavior (1987: 72).

According to Connell (1987: 76), the social constructionist approach to transsexualism can 'provide an exceptional insight into the social construction of gender in everyday life'. Garber's recent book *Vested Interests* (1993) is a useful starting point to develop this dimension. She questions whether biology has a role at all in the construction of gender:

> but if the story of transsexualism is not about sex at all, is it about subjectivity, specifically 'male subjectivity'? Does subjectivity follow the knife, or guide it? If a 'woman trapped in a man's body' is 'really' a woman, and a 'man trapped in a woman's body' is 'really' a man, what is the force of that 'really'? (1993: 109)

Put differently, Garber is raising the question of whether gender is causally prior to biological sex difference rather than biology being the essence or essential element in gender. If this is implicit to this point then it becomes more explicit as she continues:

> the phenomenon of transsexualism is both a confirmation of the construction of gender and a secondary recourse to essentialism—or, to put it a slightly different way, transsexualism demonstrates that essentialism *is* cultural construction. Nora Ephron accuses Jan Morris of essentializing stereotypes (believing in an essentializing stereotype of what a woman is). But according to what principle does she argue? That anatomy is destiny? That subjectivity follows the sign of the genitals? Or rather is she arguing that there is a difference between social construction and surgical construction, that to be a woman one needs to have been socialized as one? But if that is the case, is social construction 'natural' and surgical construction 'artificial'? (1993: 109-110, her emphasis)

Expressed serially, Garber is implicitly suggesting the causal model expressed in figure 2:1.

The idea that gender is causally prior to sex, at least among transsexuals, is new and provocative. It is provocative because it challenges the legitimacy of nature as a taken for granted standard and, at the same time, raises the difficult question of what explains gender categories if it is not sex differences. The provocation of this sort of question is important because, despite considerable interest in the notions of sex and gender over the last two decades, it is only recently that there seems to be any sophistication in how they are theorised.

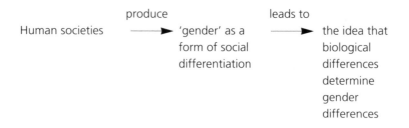

Figure 2:1   *Garber's view of the priority of gender*

The final facet of the social construction of gender is the link between sexuality and gender. By sexuality I am referring to the form and content of sexual desire. For the moment, this could be homosexual, heterosexual, asexual or bisexual and ranging from desire only to manifest sexual behaviour with others. Sexuality is not always linked to gender by social scientists (Pringle 1992: 4-5) but where the connection is made it raises profound questions about the dichotomy of gender and the contrasting continuous approach touched on by Kessler and McKenna above.

In her book on gender blending females, Holly Devor (1989) relates gender to sexuality in a reciprocal sense. On the one hand, 'gender identity for both men and women is partly defined in terms of their sexuality' but, on the other hand, 'gender dictates sexuality' in that individuals 'who see themselves as women or men must make some effort to conform to the social expectations of their gender', that is, 'sexual behavior patterns that are appropriate for members of their gender' (1989: 89). Devor uses the existence of gender blending females to illuminate the contingent nature of the gender dichotomy. Those women are females who 'project gender cues that can be socially interpreted as sufficiently masculine to earn them the social status and some of the privileges of men' (Devor 1987: 12). They see themselves as women and exhibit masculinity that leads to their being often seen as men. If 'maleness is not a necessary condition for masculinity' (Devor 1987: 34) then, when it comes to male to female transsexuals, is femaleness a necessary condition for femininity and being seen as women? Also, the more fluid approach to gender represented by gender blending females, whose gender blending is not of a medical or pathological nature, raises the question as to whether male to female transsexuals are also facets of a more complex and diverse gender picture than the dichotomous model suggests.

Claims about gender diversity prompt scrutiny of Kessler and McKenna's (1985: 163) rejection of 'dimorphism' and advocacy of a 'continuity' of gender, a stance they view as a 'paradigm change', a 'shift to seeing gender attribution as primary and gender as a practical achievement'. Their position is 'compatible' with that of Rubin (1975: 204) who, in her well-known paper 'The traffic in women', opts for the 'elimination of obligatory sexualities and sex roles' and a 'genderless society'. The principal weakness in the latter sort of claim though is that current reality is confused with the sort of genderless world hoped for. Devor (1987: 39) is similarly future oriented, expressing the sentiment 'Were people to become no longer distinguishable on the basis of sex, were all gender choices open to all humans ...': Kessler and McKenna (1985: 163) are no different when they say there is 'no necessary reason for any sort of [gender] differentiation'. All these scholars confound hope with the nature of the reality of gender categories that currently exist.[23] I do not object to the spirit behind those hopes but the reality is that what we refer to as gender seems not to be continuous but limited to a range of categories. In other words, the paradigm of gender dichotomy is being pushed to pre-revolutionary limits because of a mass of research on a variety of psychosexual identities in the contexts of homosexuality and transsexualism. The evidence suggests that, rather than gender disappearing, gender diversity is becoming more visible, especially when linked with sexual desire.

We still live in a gendered world and that includes social scientists and the people whose gender identities we study. Whether it is Devor's 'gender blending' or Kessler and McKenna's 'doing gender' and gender being a 'practical accomplishment', it is important to recognise that this sort of theorising is not eliminating notions of 'man' and 'woman'. Admittedly, we are probably talking about many categories but they are still gendered categories. When people 'do' gender, whatever the images they have of themselves, it generally includes being either a 'man' or a 'woman'. The gender blending females Devor studied saw themselves in categorical terms, for example, 'female, woman, masculine and lesbian' and, therefore, for her to say that they had personalities 'comprised of an infinitely varied, and constantly shifting, blend of what we now call gender characteristics' is, in terms of defending a *continuous* notion of gender, contradictory and, at worst, not in accord with the reality of the people she studied (Devor 1987: 38). These categories, albeit numerous and socially constructed, are more powerfully illustrated by focusing more on sexuality, specifically the interactive dimensions of desire.

Sexual desire, whether it be a state of mind and/or manifest behaviour, challenges the continuous notion of gender. Sexual desire is one facet of our being which clearly demonstrates the link between sexuality and gender, for when we desire someone and it is reciprocated, the positive nature of continuing interaction reaffirms and, possibly for some, confirms their gender identity. A male who is a masculine heterosexual man may desire a female who is a feminine heterosexual woman. If that desire is reciprocated, and continues to be reciprocated, it signals to both that they see each other in much the same way as they expect to be seen. On the other hand, if a male who is a masculine homosexual man desires another male he perceives to be an effeminate homosexual man, then that desire may be reciprocated momentarily because the latter may be a male to female transsexual who sees herself as a heterosexual feminine woman. Once she realises that the other person sees her as an effeminate man rather than a feminine woman, the desire and interaction become problematical and cannot continue without one or both redefining their gender. The homosexual man, for instance, may be bisexual and could indicate his attraction to the transsexual (male woman) as a woman. There are of course many more categories involved in sexual desire but the key point is that gender, being so integral to each of those categories, cannot be viewed as continuous. This is even illustrated by considering the bisexual man. Such a person may alternate between different categories of people he is attracted to but the one constant is that, irrespective of his partner's gender, he would always see himself as a man.

Acknowledging the link between gender and sexuality, Grimm (1987) outlines a new approach to gender based on the key point that humans relate to each other in dyads, either 'heterogenderously' or 'homogenderously' (1987: 78). This approach incorporates the many categories of sexual desire referred to earlier and her concepts of 'woman with a penis' and 'man with a vulva', for example, and the analysis of gender orientation in terms of 'erotic and non-erotic relationships' provide some idea of the number and range of categories she posits. Such categories are not qualitatively equal in most societies. As Grimm concludes, irrespective of where the 'demarcation line' of legitimate gender and sexual identity is drawn, that identity for the transsexual 'ranges further from the demarcation line than is granted even by so-called liberal standards'. Thus, 'pressure to look the way one feels or behaves seems to push transsexuals toward surgery' (1987: 81). Grimm, however, also adds that 'the transsexual (like many of us) seems to feel a discomfort with homosexuality; thus, in most cases, the transsexual seems to be heterogenderous, and altering the body satisfies this need for complementarity' (1987: 81). These categories of gender linked to sexuality raise questions about how male to female transsexuals in this study see themselves and how they are viewed by others in close personal relationships. Do their identities confirm the existence of numerous gender categories or a continuous concept of gender? Or, as some scholars posit, are they a third gender or sex? These questions will be addressed in the last two chapters.

Incorporation of the sexual dimension when considering gender also includes the body. Again, Grimm captures the point:

if we accept the argument that humans are sexual beings, then interactions between them will be affected by the morphologic gender in all contexts, because the participants are responding to stimuli about the potential for sexual behavior occurring between them or paying attention to the 'sexual' behavior that is occurring between them (1987: 82-83).

Apart from implicitly supporting the notion of 'doing gender' in interactions involving sexual desire, Grimm is stressing the point that the body, as perceived by others, is crucial. Elaborating this point a little, it is crucial because in most of those interactions the body is the first thing desired after gender has been attributed. The importance of the body in social science has been well argued by Turner (1984, 1991, 1992) and is central in theorising gender, as Connell's (1987) earlier comments indicate (see also Gatens 1983).

This mention of the body raises questions that are hardly discussed in the socio-cultural approach to transsexualism. For example, if, as Devor argues, gender and sexuality are closely linked and if gender and the body are similarly linked, then does variation in transsexuals' social backgrounds and/or social contexts have any relationship to how they see their body and its role in their living as women? Put differently, if there are variations in transsexuals' understanding of the body and its role, are those varying conceptions socially constructed? The significance of the body also raises a much more general question about its role in the maintenance of the current, narrow gender dichotomy, a question that will be considered in the final chapter.

The social construction of transsexualism

Given Grimm's approach to a new concept of gender, it is not surprising that she should support a social constructionist account of transsexualism, the third theme running through the socio-cultural literature and often closely related to the second theme, that is, the social construction of gender. Noting that gender confusion among transsexuals 'seems to be the result of various reactions to an awareness of conflict between gender identity and gender prescriptions' in a social context, 'transsexualism seems to exist primarily as a result of gender dimorphism on the part of society' (Grimm 1987: 81). The implicit assumption in this claim is that transsexuals' psychosexual identities are a part of the variety of humankind and that, faced with a rigid gender dichotomy, transsexualism is the socially tempered manifestation of those identities.

At a more macro level are Raymond's (1979) and Billings and Urban's (1982) explanation of transsexualism as a social construction. Their scope is implicit in King's (1993: 189) rendition of their 'critical' approach:

> ultimately, 'transvestism' and 'transsexualism' are products of capitalism, patriarchy or both ... Transvestism and transsexualism can be viewed as simply reflections of capitalist or patriarchal society.

For Raymond (1979: 70), it is patriarchal society that is the 'First Cause' of other causes of transsexualism. Like other analyses at this level, however, this sort of approach falters because of the constant reification of key concepts, such as patriarchy, capitalism and society, and lack of evidence. Raymond and others, such as Eichler (1980: 88), who want to reform sex stereotypes at a society level, view transsexuals as a conservative category rather than a revolutionary force in changing the structure of sex stereotypes. Given that other scholars see transsexuals as 'revolutionaries' challenging societal notions of gender (Brake 1976: 188; see also King 1993: 20), their role as revolutionary or conservative needs to be examined in the later chapters as does any evidence linking transsexualism with capitalism or patriarchy.

Concluding Comment

This review of certain categories of literature relevant to transsexualism has been selective. Its aim has been to demonstrate what we know and to identify those questions that require an answer or those that require answering from another vantage point. Clearly, vantage points influence not only the questions asked about transsexualism but also their answers, largely through research priorities and what is ultimately observed. So, within the clinical approach, for example, the assumption that transsexualism is an abnormal clinical state impinges on clinicians' concern for its aetiology and treatment. By contrast, certain feminist analyses within the socio-cultural approach spring from a perceived need to eradicate patriarchy and confound hope with the limitations of current social reality.

Among expressions of the various vantage points there is a relative silence when it comes to how transsexuals view their transsexualism. Although there are the autobiographies and the often sensational magazine articles, there is still little academic focus on transsexualism close to transsexuals' own vantage point.[24] I say 'close to' because in this book I attempt to fill that gap and, therefore, my sociological framework is superimposed over the transsexual perspectives. Of course, if it were not, one would be left with something resembling a collection of autobiographies.

From this review of the literature on transsexualism there emerge a number of issues that warrant further exploration. They include:

(a) the strong indication that gender is a process, that is, an achieved rather than an ascribed status, or a process rather than a quality;

(b) the review of literature on gender raises questions about the extent to which the widely taken for granted understanding of gender is *the* major social differentiator in all societies. Unlike other forms of social differentiation, such as ethnicity and class background, gender is widely regarded as immutable and thus the 'obvious' basis of differentiation in many areas of social life, notably the nature of the family, law,[25] work, recreation, clothes and language;[26]

(c) the notion that transsexualism is a social construction;

(d) the unrealistic rigidity of the gender dichotomy and the question of whether transsexuals are a third gender or are a part of a more complex picture of psychosexual identities that have hitherto been invisible;

(e) the link between sexual orientation and gender;

(f) the greater visibility of male to female transsexuals, both in reality and media coverage of it; and

(g) the question of whether transsexuals are a revolutionary affront to gender or reinforcers of gender stereotypes.

All these will be examined in the following chapters.

In addition, there are some residual issues worth identifying because they also raise questions for consideration in the later chapters. For instance, given the recent prominence of the sociological significance of the body, there is a relative silence in the literature on the social significance of the body in analyses of transsexualism. This prompts a careful examination of transsexuals' own accounts of the importance of the body at various stages in their transsexual careers. Also, the issue of gender as continuous or categorised warrants further consideration, as does the claim that all gender classifications are contingent on social factors. Drawing on anthropological research, for example, the suggestion that transsexuals may be the western counterparts of the berdache would be overlooking this caution about contingency. Apart from other difficulties this suggestion might pose, it would be a case of imposing one gender schema—an unfamiliar trichotomous one—on top of the familiar dichotomous model. If gender is contingent on social factors, then the question of what maintains the rigidity of the dichotomous model is another question worthy of more attention.

Finally, because this examination of the literature has been selective rather than comprehensive, it does not present a complete picture of the transsexual located in an everyday social context. Therefore, to complete this preamble to our consideration of the macro and micro aspects of becoming a woman in chapters four and five, the following chapter provides a glimpse of the personal history of Miranda—a transsexual.

NOTES

1 For a general view of the literature on transsexualism, see Bolin (1987a, 1987b). See also Denny (1994) and the bibliographies in each of the contributions in Walters and Ross (1986) which provide a cross section of the clinical literature.

2 The list of works by male to female transsexuals is relatively lengthy when compared to those written by female to male transsexuals. Concerning the former, see, for example, Cowell (1954); Sinclair (1965); Jorgenson (1968); Fry (1974); Canary (1974); Fallowell and Ashley (1982); Richards (1983); Grant (1983); Morris (1987); Cossey (1991); Cummings (1992). For shorter but nevertheless autobiographical works, see also Wells (1986) and the memoirs of Herculine Barbin (Foucault 1980). For female to male transsexual autobiographies, see Stirling (1989) and Johnson and Brown (1982), which is an autobiography by two married transsexuals, one female to male and the other male to female.

3 Jan Morris notes that she has read only one novel dealing with 'gender confusion', which is Geoff Brown's *I Want What I Want*. There are at least two others in existence—Rose Tremaine's *The Sacred Country* and Leslie Feinberg's *Stonebutch Blues: A Novel*.

4 See the comment in chapter one concerning the practical difficulties of gaining a representative sample of transsexuals.

5 *New Idea* (1989) 22 April: 12–13. See also, for example, 'Women who want to be men', *New Woman* (1993) March: 46–49; 'My son is now my daughter', *Woman's Day* (1993) 22 November: 36–37; and 'The trauma of being a transsexual', *Woman's Day* (1988) 26 April: 25–27.

6 Bolin (1987a: 41), with whom I concur, notes that 'clinical' covers medical, psychiatric and psychological research because of the focus on transsexualism in each of those disciplines as something requiring 'treatment and observation'.

7 For a longer discussion of the history of transsexualism, see Bullough (1975, 1976a, 1976b). See also King (1981).

8 Ross (1986b: 24-2); Walters (1988: 24, 27).

9 Burnard and Ross (1986: 52-53); Harding (1986: 114, 115, 121).

10 Walters (1988: 28); see also Wells (1986: 13) and Harding (1986: 115).

11 See Ross (1986b: 20); Wells (1986: 10); Green (1974); Riseley (1986: 30); Bower (1986: 44); and Walters (1988: 22-23).

12 Ross (1986b: 21); Burnard and Ross (1986: 54).

13 References to the gaps in knowledge about the aetiology of transsexualism and/or its likely multi-causal nature appear in a variety of sources; see, for example, Ross (1986a, 1986b); Riseley (1986: 26); Walters (1988: 21-27); *Lancet* (1991: 603); Docter (1988: v, 57, 65); Hodgkinson (1987: 28); Goh (1991: 15-16, 19); and Tsoi (1991: 31). See also Laub and Gandy (1973); Money (1968) and Money and Ehrhardt (1972).

14 'Nature', as Goh uses the term, corresponds to Docter's (1988: 1-2) biological/medical approach to transvestism and transsexualism and includes organic influences, such as neurophysiological, hormonal and genetic factors. 'Nurture' covers both Docter's 'intrapsychic/psychodynamic' and 'developmental/learning' models. In the former, Docter refers to the dynamics of personality development in infancy, whereas the latter covers the process of learning and socialisation.

15 For further literature on the different arguments surrounding pseudo-hermaphrodites in the Dominican Republic, see Imperato-McGinley *et al.* (1979); Money (1976); Herdt (1990).

16 On a theoretical point, even in King's 'orientation model', 'pathology *is* attributed to the transsexual' (1984: 45, his emphasis). More explicitly, the 'condition model views it as an illness' (1984: 47). In the latter model, the strong assumption of pathology invites intervention. This is evident in Socarides' view of transsexuals, a view King quotes:

> The fact that the transsexual cannot accept his sex as anatomically outlined ... is a sign of the intense emotional and mental disturbance which exists within him. It is the emotional disturbance which must be attacked through suitable means by psychotherapy which provides alleviation of anxiety and psychological retraining rather than amputation or surgery (1984: 47).

17 For example, estimates of the prevalence of male to female transsexualism in the Netherlands range from one in 11,900 to one in 20,000 males and for female to male transsexuals, one in 30,400 to one in 50,000 females (cf. Bakker *et al.* 1993 and Eklund *et al.* 1988). On the prevalence of transsexualism in Australia, see Walters (1988: 27); Riseley (1986: 26); Burnard and Ross (1986: 52-53); Townsend (1978: 28); and Lopez (1991: 18).

18 Transsexualism as a diagnosis has come under critical scrutiny by Tully (1992: 4), who refers to the related terms 'primary and secondary' transsexualism as 'perhaps the most precarious subclassification'.

19 Bolin is quoting from pp.112-120 of Kessler and McKenna.

20 It is of interest to note that Money claims for himself the distinction of generating the notion of 'gender'. 'The need to find an umbrella term', as he says, was 'imperative in the early 1950s ... That is why I turned to philology and linguistics and borrowed the term, gender' (1988: 53).

21 For a critique of theorising on the concepts of sex and gender that overlooks the body, see Gatens (1983).

22 For cross cultural literature relevant to transsexualism, see the discussion in Bolin (1987a: 52-58); Kessler and McKenna (1985: 21-41); Green (1974: 3-13); and Money (1988: 89, 93, 98-100). A selection of more general, cross cultural research includes Wikan (1977); Creed (1984); Herdt (1989); Lindenbaum (1984); and Whitam (1987). For specific works on the berdache, see Blackwood (1984); Callendar and Kochems (1983); Forgey (1975); Fulton and Anderson (1992); Greenberg (1985); Thayer (1980); and Williams (1985).

23 See chapter six for further discussion of analysis based on hope.

24 'Academic' is not used loosely but, rather, specifies the critical and/or explanatory dimensions that social scientists, for example, attempt to add to empirical findings. Stuart's (1983) study, for example, is close to transsexuals' own vantage point but lacks an explanatory/critical perspective.

25 See, for example, Finlay (1988).

26 See Woodhouse (1989: 7, 9-16). In her discussion of clothes and language there is an insightful comment on the role of pronouns.

3
Miranda

There were no guests or presents at Miranda's 'fifth birthday', but then it was not an ordinary birthday. This was a solitary and symbolic occasion. Miranda, a successful, thirty-six year-old office manager in a large company, was privately acknowledging the fifth anniversary of her transition from Michael to Miranda. The past five years living full time as a woman had had their ups and downs but, on reflection, Miranda felt they had been worthwhile. There had been the odd bad experience, but that was insignificant alongside all those years spent as Michael. A part of the symbolic nature of this occasion was that it reaffirmed not only Miranda's need to make a new start in life, but also having achieved it. Perhaps not surprisingly she had difficulty reflecting on the past but, given the increasingly more comfortable vantage point of the present, it was easier now for Miranda to let her mind wander.

Growing Up

Miranda's earliest recollection was that period just before she, as Michael, was about to start school. As the only child in the family at that time, Michael's playmates were four neighbourhood girls he met at the local preschool. The five children were very close and often spent weekends and vacations away with each other's families. Miranda often looks back on that period with nostalgia and wonders whether the same bonds and feelings could ever exist again if they all were brought together. A part of that nostalgia is her recollection that, at the time, Michael was happy and being 'Michael' was not something he had to think about. He assumed everyone, that is, all preschoolers, were like himself. Starting school was to be more problematical.

The years of primary school coincided with the waning of the comfortable relationships Michael had with the girls. It was not that he felt any different towards them: it was more the anxiety that entered an increasingly complex life. The first anxious moment followed an incident not long after Michael started school. He was punished by his teacher for accompanying the girls into the toilet. Michael's mother tried to explain why he could not continue sharing the same toilet. Miranda still remembers her mother kneeling down and saying 'Michael, you can't go into the girls' toilets because you're not a girl'.

That incident was the first of many in which Michael was reprimanded for not doing what was expected of boys. He was kept apart from his friends and constantly reminded that he was a boy: 'boys could not play in the girls' section of the playground' and 'boys could not sit next to girls in class'. Being told he was a boy and not a girl challenged Michael's non-gendered view of the world. He was told that boys had a penis and girls did not. The importance adults placed on this difference had not occurred to Michael before. He was aware of what they were referring to when stressing the significance of male and female genitals but, up to that point, had not thought much about it. Penis or no penis was like having long hair or short hair and certainly had nothing to do with being 'one of the girls'. Children were children and the terms 'boys' and 'girls' were just ways in which adults distinguished one group of children from another. After all, he was fond of hearing from his own and friends' parents that he was 'one of the girls' but was now aware of others treating him as a 'boy'. Anxiety and confusion were the vehicles of Michael's introduction to a gendered world.

As a young child, Michael had no counter for what he was constantly hearing, that having male genitals and looking like a boy meant that he was a boy and not a girl. His parents' certainty of this fact, especially his mother's reassuring words that had always calmed his childhood confusions, and the daily boy–girl socialisation at school slowly consolidated Michael's acknowledgement that he was a boy. What else could he be? As the primary school years passed, though, whatever level of acknowledgement that may have existed was replaced with increasing uneasiness.

For the young Michael, the principal source of confusion alongside his public persona of being a boy was his abiding feeling of preferring to be with his friends—the girls. He preferred their company, their activities, and had no interest in boys' activities, especially sport. His confusion was only deepened by his private hope that some day he would become a girl. He realised that the feelings of his preschool years of being like and wanting to be with the girls were not shared by all boys his age. At night he would lie awake and wish that he could be suddenly turned into a girl. The lack of fulfilment of that often repeated wish was accompanied by his growing envy of girls and the feeling that something had been denied him. At the same time, anxiety was the price of Michael's lack of enthusiasm for the usual array of boys' activities. He was constantly being blamed for his lack of effort in physical education classes resulting in loss of team games. For not being like the other boys—that is, being an aggressive participant in sports, being prepared to fight to settle playground disputes, and celebrating getting dirty—he was subjected to a variety of teasing and bullying. Being called a 'sissy' was mild compared to the ambushes after school when numbers of boys would corner him on the way home and provoke a fight. School was not a positive experience for Michael.

It was during those primary school years, when he was eight years of age, that Michael began secretly to dress in his mother's clothes. Although opportunities were rare and despite his mother's clothes being far too large, those occasions felt right. They are still among the more vivid, positive memories Miranda has of childhood, despite what followed when Michael's mother discovered his secret activity. She had suspected for some time that he had been doing something with her clothes because she had noticed on several occasions that her underclothes and stockings had been disturbed. Michael felt humiliated when his mother confronted him with the truth. If an adequate explanation existed, then he certainly was not aware of it. The cross dressing persisted, however, and so did the severity of the punishment. In desperation, Michael's confused parents took him to a psychiatrist. Many years later, after her reassignment surgery, Miranda learned of the significance those psychiatric consultations had for her parents. It was not so much the difficulty of going outside the family with what they had come to regard as 'Michael's problem' but, rather, their slow discovery that that problem was no mere passing, psychological whim. Michael's problem, whatever its cause, was real and was here to stay. They could see that although he was perfectly normal in every other respect, chances were that he might never be like the boys in his class. Those boys played sport, enjoyed each other's company, and participated in a daily round of rough and tumble. Michael, by contrast, was everything they were not. He was certainly not interested in sport. Also, he was a loner and disliked getting dirty. Part of the significance they attached to Michael's increasing social isolation and persistent cross dressing was their own private concern about his future. They, however, could never have imagined his eventual destination.

It was not until twenty years after those psychiatric consultations that they eventually were able to discuss their concerns with Miranda. Their confusion and reluctance to confront Michael with their anxieties, even when he was much older, were mainly a result of the inconclusive nature of the psychiatric tests. Hence, they were unable to put a label on the 'problem', which only fuelled their uncertainty. In any case, it was not their way of doing things to discuss their concerns with their children, least of all in this case. With solid working class origins, Michael's father, then a builder, and his mother, a housewife all her married life, were stoical but inwardly in need of emotional support. They were convinced by the time Michael was eleven years of age that he would never grow up to be a normal boy. The strange thing was that, years later, when they eventually opened up to Miranda, they had difficulty pinning down what sort of normal boy they had expected Michael to be.

Puberty and Adolescence

By the time Michael had reached high school, teasing and bullying by class mates had developed into indifference and social
isolation. The lack of even a few acquaintances meant that school
had become something to be endured and was anything but an
enjoyable experience. Michael's school work suffered. The
nagging confusion surrounding feeling different and not being
able to discuss it with anyone for fear of exacerbating the ridicule
and rejections were a constant distraction in class and made application to academic achievement extremely difficult. Moreover,
poor performance increased Michael's already low self-esteem,
especially when he was punished in front of the whole class. On
many of those occasions he was physically unable to answer the
teacher's intimidating questions, which only led to more degrad-
ing public punishment.

Over the following two or three years Michael settled into an
uneasy accommodation with life. It was uneasy because, on the
one hand, he knew he was a boy but, on the other, he experienced the emotional warmth of fantasising being a girl. These
two states of mind sat awkwardly together. There was, however,
an accommodation of sorts that was not a result of any conscious
decision making but more an acceptance of the day to day
routine of feeling uncomfortable. Michael had come to take his
situation for granted. He had no choices: he was a boy with no
friends who lived a routine existence alternating between home
and school. 'Wasn't this fairly normal?' he often thought. At
the same time though he also wondered 'Are there other boys
like me?'

Following the brief period of contact with the psychiatrist,
Michael realised it was not worth risking 'going public' by
expressing his fantasies. This applied especially to cross dressing,
which he continued to do but ever so carefully to avoid being
caught again by his parents. It also applied to displaying his everyday, vague feeling of anxiety and depression. Previously, his overt
moodiness and depression triggered a verbal frenzy from his
parents. Their angry and anxious claims that 'We knew you didn't

get straightened out through that psychiatric treatment', 'I still think there's something not quite right in that head of yours', and 'You and your little hang-ups have certainly given us the run around' had a repetitious ring about them. By now Michael had learned to put up a good front for his parents and others. He hid his feelings and cultivated a bright, chatty exterior. It worked to the extent that his parents hardly ever raised the issue of Michael's old 'problem'. The masquerade clearly seemed to satisfy their understanding of what a 'normal' boy was. Michael's pragmatism provided yet another reason to lie awake at night and ponder his fantasies. The problem was that everyday life felt artificial whereas his fantasy of being a girl felt real and normal.

The emotionally flat and uneventful nature of the early teens started to change some months before Michael turned fifteen. Puberty had started. At first he did not take much notice of the wavering tone and occasional shrill in his voice, but when facial hair started to appear along with other bodily changes, he became increasingly distressed. His gain in height, increasing muscularity, needing to shave, if only occasionally, and a more stable deep voice were salient for Michael, not so much as a signal of adult-hood but because of the imminence of becoming a man. He had not thought much about growing up, perhaps because he did not want to, but he still could not understand why he felt distressed. How could he explain it? He knew he was a boy but he did not want to be a man because he had always wanted to be a girl. Nevertheless, he was distressed over slowly losing his slender, slight physique, his babyish complexion, and his soft voice. In the privacy of his own mind he constantly tossed the questions around. Did puberty signal the real situation, that there was absolutely no point in hoping, even though it was fantasy, that some day he might become a woman? Did the prospect of becoming a man mean that he could not, or should not, even fantasise about being a girl or, rather, a woman? Puberty brought with it no rewards. Feelings of unease and depression persisted, especially when Michael started having spontaneous erections and the occasional wet dream. His parents could not be 'kept off the scent' by his usual feigned, chirpy behaviour. They noticed his change of temperament and mood but put it down to puberty and the pressure of school work. They did not raise the point.

Nothing was ever said.

The mid-teen years were the most difficult Michael had ever faced in his short life. In looking back now, Miranda wonders how she ever coped with that particular phase of growing up. Life during primary and early high school years were not easy but they were merely inconvenient compared to those few years after puberty. Continuous unease developed into constant anxiety. It was possibly this anxiety that prevented Michael from discussing with his mother what had become a serious problem. He could discuss most things with her but not this matter. Feelings of self-doubt, confusion and depression surrounding what he was supposed to feel about being a young man had reached the point where he could do nothing. Michael felt that his mother could not possibly understand what he was feeling if he confessed to her that he had a deep longing to be a girl. He could rationalise it by saying that this was merely a fantasy but there are good reasons for having persistent fantasies, and why was Michael having these fantasies? On the other hand, he could say nothing and pretend that everyone who went through puberty had stresses and strains. The problem was that he knew that what he was experiencing was no ordinary confusion of growing up. No one else he knew was experiencing such obvious torment. Or were they? How would he know? Perhaps the only built-in protection to Michael's sanity at that stage, and therefore the very condition that allowed him to put one year in front of the other, was that he had no resources to change his situation. He might have taken himself off to some other city in search of answers if he had had money and knowledge of the whys and wherefores of the world.

Despite Michael's low state there was something significant about that period in his life. Even today Miranda can remember her changing feelings at that time. Looking back she is very clear that shortly before her seventeenth birthday she saw that fantasy was reality: she wanted to live as a woman because she was a woman. Hindsight though has a way of simplifying and compressing events. For Michael, coping with the conviction was more protracted. It was a complex matter to know that he was not a boy, that he did not want to be a man, and that he could not be happy in himself unless he could somehow acknowledge that he was really a developing woman. With the onset of secondary sexual characteristics, it was as if he had to declare himself now or risk going further and further away from his ideal, perhaps going over the edge forever.

Apart from the daily reminder of a developing male body, which was upsetting, there were increasingly difficult situations at school that confirmed Michael's conviction. He was experiencing growing embarrassment at having to undress in front of boys during school sports sessions. He had always been a little coy about nakedness and was never one to frolic in the showers with other boys. Now, however, it was not so much embarrassment about changes associated with puberty, such as his rapid growth of pubic hair, but rather the feeling of being a woman who was forced to undress in public. Having male genitals had little to do with his embarrassment, for although Michael disliked and, in the past, had loathed them, he tried to block out those feelings by refusing to admit they existed.

About a year later, when Michael was in his last year of high school, he made a significant discovery. He was visiting his local doctor and in the waiting room happened to read a magazine article about a transsexual, a man who underwent surgery and became a woman. The sequence of events and, more important, the person's feelings were identical to his in every respect, although Michael had not heard the term 'transsexual' before. What he had thought was his own private and somewhat idiosyncratic life to that point was now replicated in every detail by someone else and, more to the point, was being made public in a popular women's magazine. Fantasy started to fade. Michael now had an immense sense of confidence in the reality of his own feelings. Even if only one other person felt the same way, it meant that Michael's *problem* was not just *Michael's* problem. He had made a profound discovery.

In the following year Michael learned all he could about transsexualism. He travelled to the city library to read as much as possible on the subject, especially the few biographies of well-known transsexuals. Even though anxiety about his own gender had not diminished, there was a strong positive note to life following the discovery of transsexualism. Even though the literature estimated one in fifty to a hundred thousand people was a transsexual, the possibility of being able to follow the path of others in the same predicament was the most positive and challenging thought he had had in years.

At this time Michael made the transition from school to work. He did not have the choice of going to university because his anxieties over the preceding years had been a constant distraction and, consequently, his school work had suffered. With more luck than ability he obtained a job as an office clerk in a large company in the city. Although the work was not very interesting, its monotony did not pose a problem because nobody really seemed to notice Michael or make demands on him. This job suited his socially isolated lifestyle and provided one additional benefit. It gave him the income to buy the women's clothes he had previously only been able to admire. Unfortunately, time and a place to cross dress were not as forthcoming because he still lived at home.

Some months later, after having saved a little money, Michael moved into a modest apartment. It did not need to be spacious, for he lived alone and hardly anyone would be visiting. This presented the opportunity to cross dress in the clothes he wanted to wear all the time. Despite limited opportunities in the past, cross dressing no longer presented any erotic pleasure. It was more a source of inner calm and, consequently, on most evenings and weekends Michael dressed as a woman. He would often stand in front of a mirror and wonder about what he saw. His reflections pleased him, that is, apart from his male genitals. Increasingly, Michael treated them with indifference. When showering, for instance, he would handle his penis and scrotum as little as possible and, at home, would sit to urinate. He knew that reassignment surgery, some day, would remove his cause for concern.

Adulthood—Early Years

Some years passed before Michael felt he must do something about what he had to that point only hoped for There were reasons for his lack of action. First, he was not sure what the first step should be. Approaching his local doctor seemed the obvious starting point but, despite his presumption that all doctors had a strong sense of confidentiality, he was uneasy about his parents finding out. That doctor had been the family doctor for many years and saw Michael's parents regularly. What if he happened to let slip that he had seen Michael recently? That would be an awkward situation and Michael was not good at lying. Another reason for not doing anything was that Michael knew from his reading on transsexualism that gender reassignment surgery was expensive, not to mention the cost of other services such as electrolysis to remove facial hair. Until he had some capital he could do nothing.

By his early twenties Michael had saved a few thousand dollars. Even though he now had the means to pay for whatever gender reassignment surgery might cost, he still had a certain inertia, a reluctance to make a definite move. He could see more clearly that he faced a massive dilemma. On the one hand, he wanted desperately to live as a woman all the time, not just part time as he had been doing. On the other hand, he wanted to make the change without anyone knowing about it, especially his parents and the people he worked with. It was more than a dilemma for Michael: it was a contradiction. He could *not* make the change without their knowing. This was an important insight because he could see that for the last few years he was using lack of money as an excuse for not doing anything. The painful admission was accepting that lack of courage, not money, was the obstacle.

Michael resolved to do something. With less sensitivity concerning the consequences of approaching his local doctor, he finally made an appointment. He unloaded his history of gender confusion and associated anxiety to his doctor, who arranged a referral to a gender clinic at a major city hospital. His doctor was supportive, saying in passing that he had suspected 'something like this' for years. As the referral letter to the gender clinic was being scribbled, Michael noted the key paragraph, which read:

Michael has a long history of self-identification as a woman. He has strong feelings about wanting to live as a woman and wants to proceed to surgery to change his sex. For your assessment please.

Although the first round of contacts with the clinic was uneventful, the future was not as rosy as Michael had anticipated. To begin with, he was not told one way or the other whether the clinic would go ahead with reassignment surgery. The whole process was far more protracted than he had assumed. He was to be kept under observation for an indefinite period of time and, on top of this, would have to live full time as a woman before surgery could even be considered. Clearly, there were no guarantees. During this period of contact with the clinic he was put in touch with a transsexual support group, where he met other people who were at different points along the path of making the transition to living full time as women. Although he was later to discover that there were female to male transsexuals, at the time he placed little significance on their absence in the support group.

Over the following year Michael routinely kept his appointments with the specialists associated with the gender clinic. Not knowing whether he would be recommended for surgery and, if so, when was unsettling. This uncertainty only added to the pessimistic interpretation he placed on the results of his routine psychological tests. He seemed to dwell on isolated phrases, such as 'testing shows that he still identifies more with masculine rather than feminine images', and placed far more significance on the tests than was warranted. At this time he met two women who seemed to halt the momentum he had gathered in his transition. Of course, looking back now Miranda can see that meeting those women was the last straw in a process of rising doubt about the whole process of changing gender but they were to be of immense significance. The first woman was Nadine, another transsexual, who was also a member of the transsexual support group. The other woman was Jillian, whom Michael fell in love with.

Nadine was about Michael's age but had been living full time as a woman for about five years. She had been on female hormones for the same period, having first taken her mother's oral contraceptive tablets and then later, on medical advice, the appropriate daily dose of synthetic estrogen. She had been attending the same gender clinic as Michael for two years and expected to be recommended for surgery within a year, depending on the availability of the limited public funding for reassignment surgery. Nadine had no money, no job, little education and few prospects for the future, yet was confident that after her operation everything would 'pick up'. What bothered Michael was Nadine's unrealistic grasp of her own situation. He knew he had experienced years of anxiety and depression and sometimes wondered whether he himself had a proper grasp of reality, but Nadine was completely out of touch. He could see that even if a person were not a transsexual, if they were as lacking in social skills and resources as Nadine was it was virtually a disability for life. In addition, she had no one to turn to for support. She was thrown out of home by her father and told not to return while she persisted in her 'sick and perverted' lifestyle. Her father had even put a shotgun to her head to emphasise the point.

Just knowing Nadine forced Michael to rehearse in his mind what he might have to go through when he confronted his parents. He knew they were caring and would never reject him, as Nadine's had. Or would they? His father could get very stirred up about certain issues and Michael had already heard him sounding off about what should be done to 'cure once and for all' the rising number of homosexuals. Michael could not absorb Nadine's situation and tried to distance himself from it because he was already very depressed over the longer than expected wait he might have for surgery. He constantly thought of Nadine though and saw himself, as if in a mirror. Was he deceiving himself that he could make the transition to living as a woman? Could he just simply tell his parents that he had always seen himself inside as a woman and was going to make that change? Did he really think they could get their minds and emotions around the notion of reassignment surgery? He began to imagine his father exploding and trying to deflect the issue by saying 'It just indicates how messed up you really are. Who in his right mind would *ask* to have his penis cut off?' Michael knew they could not cope. If they could not cope, then why was he persisting with the whole notion of making the transition to being a woman? Was it just an indication of how unrealistic he really was? Was he really any different from Nadine? He had started out attending the gender clinic with enthusiasm and, later, had become depressed about the prospect of a long wait for surgery. Now he had sunk even lower by wondering whether he should take the easier option, that is, give up the gender clinic and the whole idea of reassignment surgery.

At that time, as if the jolt prompted by Nadine were not enough, Jillian entered Michael's life. They met through an acquaintance in the company Michael worked for. At first, he found her pleasant to talk to and, given his shy, withdrawn manner, wondered why she found him such good company. That might have been just a chance encounter except that over the next few weeks he found himself regularly meeting Jillian at a local supermarket where they both shopped. She initiated going beyond polite conversation by first inviting him to have coffee at a nearby coffee shop. Later, she followed with an invitation to lunch.

During this period Michael enjoyed Jillian's company. He felt relaxed and began to take the initiative by telephoning her to arrange meetings. For the first time in his adult life he consciously felt an attraction to another person. She, for a time, took his mind off the depression and confusion that followed in the wake of his acquaintance with Nadine.

The joy of being with Jillian seemed to neutralise Michael's growing anxiety over his increasing physical attraction to her. He was beginning to worry about how he could feel this way at the same time as having had all those feelings about becoming a woman. He knew he could not possibly discuss this confusion with Jillian. If he could not make sense of the confusion then what might her response be? Eventually, Michael and Jillian reached a level of physical intimacy where passion outweighed restraint. Following attempted intercourse, Michael was more surprised at having reached such a level of physical closeness than being worried about his impotence. Jillian had not minded, adding that it often happened to men who were having sex for the first time. On the second and third occasions of attempted intercourse and impotence, however, Michael was distressed. Being sexually attracted to Jillian posed enough of a dilemma in light of his previous convictions about his transsexualism. Being unable to go through with it was punishing.

Jillian was patient though. Her calmness and good company kept Michael happy and reasonably relaxed. Talking together about the unimportance of high levels of sexual performance, Michael felt reassured. He noticed but did not dwell on Jillian's comment that she felt as if Michael sometimes responded to her as a sister. Some months later, Michael managed to have inter-course with Jillian. It was more uneventful than planned. After a pleasant dinner at her apartment they found themselves in bed without reflecting too much on their previous lack of success. The following day Michael could not understand what had been wrong about the previous night. Yet, they had both felt very close and it was something Michael wanted to repeat.

After the next intimate encounter, Michael realised what was wrong. He saw what had been missing before. With the benefit of less alcohol he found himself wanting to be passionate towards Jillian and wanting her to respond to him, but as if he were a woman. Those old feelings Michael thought were waning came flooding back. Sex with Jillian was good, but it was good because he felt as if he were also a woman. He did not want to be pene-trated, nor did he want to penetrate Jillian. Some months later, Michael and Jillian's relationship ended. Despite many long, tor-menting discussions about each other's feelings, Michael had only skirted the issue of wanting to be a woman. Several years later she would hear the full story.

In looking back at that relationship, one of the positive out-comes for Miranda was that it gave her the first experience of the joy of being close to another person. It also clarified that the object of her desire was another woman, although, in the few years following that traumatic parting from Jillian, this conviction was filed away in the recesses of Michael's mind.

The culmination of Michael's experiences with Nadine and Jillian seemed to shift his whole sense of direction. He stopped attending the gender clinic in the belief that he was really a psy-chologically confused male. He also began attending gay clubs, believing that, possibly, he had never been honest with himself. The casual, gay sexual encounters that inevitably occurred proved disastrous. Michael's high expectations of what those encounters might mean were unfulfilled. He felt used and abused, a con-venient sexual object who was last of all a person. It did not take long for him to realise that he was definitely not gay. He was not yet capable though of challenging his identity, albeit wavering, of being a man.

In the belief that he was not gay and, therefore, must be a heterosexual man, Michael set about demonstrating it by joining the part time army reserve. What better way was there of showing that he was a man? He knew the army wanted 'real' men who enjoyed outdoor, physical activities. It certainly did not accept wimps! At first, the army seemed beneficial. Not only was he able to do some advanced courses that strengthened skills he used in his day job, but he also seemed to benefit from the male company he met. Other part time soldiers seemed to like him and included him in their activities, which reinforced Michael's understanding of himself as a man.

Had it not been for the heavy drinking, Michael might not have lasted in the army. Those old feelings surrounding wanting to be a woman would often loom and on numerous camps he was aware of developing cunning strategies to avoid being naked in front of others in the showers. Any anxieties he had were always cured by a few drinks. This sort of heavy drinking was not confined to camp life. The army had been a good training ground for a number of activities and heavy binge drinking had become a private pastime for Michael after work at night. The point of no return was close. During a summer vacation and shortly after his thirtieth birthday he would have had no way of knowing that binge would be his last.

Michael woke to find a nurse taking his pulse. Why was he in hospital? His doctor explained that he was admitted two days earlier with acute alcoholic poisoning. A neighbour had heard Michael moaning and called an ambulance. He might have died had he not been admitted to hospital. Michael took this news calmly at first but later that day found himself spontaneously crying. He could not stop. Some days later he confronted the reality of his life and his options. He had to admit to himself that for years he had been trying to deny wanting to live as a woman. He felt he had run out of excuses. There was no serious financial limitation to reassignment surgery. He had been on the gender clinic program before, so he could not say that he was unaware of it. His own shame and low self-esteem were the real obstacles.

Before he had found the thought of telling his parents about his true feelings and expectations excruciating. Now, if he did not confront this hurdle, then an even worse option could loom. He might not be around to be able to worry about it.

Adulthood—A New Direction

The staff of the gender clinic saw a different Michael when he rejoined the program. His parents now knew the whole story and, although initially shocked, were unexpectedly accepting and supportive. Their support and his own firm realisation of his need to live as a woman led to some definite decisions. He decided to make the change after people at work were appropriately informed. A work counsellor in the company was one of the first colleagues Michael told. She suggested he take a short period of leave. While he was away she would inform all sections of the company of his decision to live as a woman and would provide them with the basic knowledge about transsexualism.

Michael had thought a lot about a new name. He decided that when *he* returned to work *she* would be Miranda. In preparation for the transition Michael took the necessary steps to have his name changed by deed poll. At the same time he applied to have his driver's licence, Medicare card, and other documents reissued in the name of Miranda.

Within three months of leaving hospital Michael returned to work as Miranda. The transition was less harrowing than she imagined. People were polite and often a little awkward, but there was widespread respect for Miranda's courage and conviction. The work counsellor's efforts had smoothed the way in many ways. It was obvious that providing information on transsexualism had given them some idea of what to expect but it was also the sorting out beforehand of small but significant matters. Which toilet, for example, would Miranda use? Most colleagues were comfortable with the idea of Miranda using the female toilets but a few were troubled by Miranda still being a pre-operative transsexual. The decision to allow Miranda to use a toilet that required a key for access was a welcome compromise that posed no difficulties for anyone.

The months passed and Miranda found her work colleagues routinely accepting her as 'Miranda'. That felt good. There were no jokes or insults, at least not to her face. Even after this relatively short period as Miranda, she felt life was a much more enjoyable affair. With new confidence she resumed contact with the transsexual support group and was well under way with a routine program of electrolysis to remove facial hair permanently. It was expensive and, above all, required perseverance, but that did not matter. Her new life was assuming its own history. The day she started to live as Miranda was day one, and she was counting. The past was beginning to fade, something that Miranda, perhaps somewhat symbolically, hastened by destroying all her old photographs and school books. Her life had really just begun.

Miranda wondered whether her feelings of contentment and well being might be a result of the female hormones that she had been routinely taking for several months. She was aware that her body was responding in other ways to the synthetic hormones. Apart from the occasional mood swing her weight redistribution was noticeable. She was developing more rounded hips and losing bulk around her arms and shoulders. Breast development was beginning, but had a long way to go Miranda thought, and her skin generally felt softer and smoother. Even her penis and testes were noticeably smaller and erections had ceased altogether. She thought, perhaps, the genitals might disappear altogether.

On her first anniversary of living as a woman, her first 'birthday', Miranda reflected on the previous year and jotted a few thoughts in her diary:

I am generally happy to be a woman—at last. I couldn't go back to living as … I don't want to write the name. Even if I couldn't some day have the operation, I would still want to live as I am now.

She knew life as Miranda had not been perfect. There had been a few incidents that had been upsetting but in hindsight they were trivial. On one occasion, for example, a bank teller had asked 'Can I help you, sir?' He apologised when he realised his mistake but it upset Miranda. She thought 'Was it because I was dressed in jeans and a sloppy shirt and looked sort of unisex? Or was it because I really didn't look like a woman?' There had also been a couple of incidents at work. A few words were exchanged when Miranda challenged two older women she overheard sniggering about her being an 'artificial woman'. She also had a similar exchange with a man in the storeroom, who made some comment about her not being worthy of a wolf whistle. Generally though, she felt as if she had fared relatively well in being seen and treated as a woman. Others in the support group had had a more traumatic transition.

On this occasion she also reflected on her parents' responses over the past year. Although they were really not completely accepting of her transition to Miranda, they had been extremely supportive and caring. She realised support was not distributed equally among transsexuals in recalling the images of Nadine's parents. She had not seen her old friend for years. 'What has become of her?' she wondered. Associating one thought with another, the same questions about Jillian came to mind. Miranda would soon find out.

By the end of the following year Miranda was almost thirty-three. She was confident the gender clinic would recommend her for reassignment surgery because on more than one occasion staff openly discussed their views with her. She knew she had all the good prognostic indicators. There were no signs of major psychopathology. She had a long history of seeing herself and wanting to live as a woman, accompanied by a similarly long history of cross dressing. Although not as young as some others who were anticipating surgery, she had acknowledged being transsexual at an early age, and had always been regarded as a somewhat effeminate loner. Also, she had a relatively low sex drive, a slight build and, currently, had good support from family, a few friends and work colleagues.

Up to this point, Miranda's experience of the gender clinic had been positive. She was aware from some of her contacts at the transsexual support group that not all transsexuals shared her views about the clinic. Some had found staff intimidating. One or two, for example, had confessed to Miranda that they were full of self-doubt about their gender identity. Their sessions with certain staff were difficult and they were having second thoughts about going on. Miranda put a different slant on this sort of situation. Anyone who contemplated anything as profound as reassignment surgery needed to have their assumptions tested, and tested vigorously.

A common belief among members of the support group was that during consultations with clinic staff they had to be careful not to touch on their own feelings about anything that might be regarded as a bit kinky, especially anything to do with their sex lives. They assumed staff were acting as censors of transsexuals wanting reassignment surgery. Mention of any departure from the 'straight and narrow', such as being a lesbian, might delay or prevent their being recommended for surgery. Miranda thought this problem was more apparent than real. As if the clinic staff did not know the game some people were playing! After all, Miranda knew that she was attracted to women but this had not been a problem, given that staff had positive views about her being a good candidate for surgery. In any case this assumption would soon be put to the test because she was to hear shortly whether the clinic would recommend her for surgery.

Miranda's confidence was borne out. Two months after being notified that reassignment surgery had been approved, her operation was performed at a private hospital. This moment was something of an anticlimax. The significance this sort of surgery had when she first discovered transsexualism was now not there. It was marvellous to have reached this point but the operation was just another stage in the process of becoming a woman.

During the six weeks of post-operative recuperation, Miranda spent many hours reflecting on her past and her future. New priorities were now replacing old ones. She was conscious of being more relaxed about the necessity of looking feminine at all times. In those early months of living as a woman she remembers feeling the urgency of having to look 'right' on all occasions. Miranda could now laugh at the ridiculous situations this obsession got her into, such as receiving friendly jibes at the corner store when she went for a carton of milk at eight in the morning in a party dress. She knew she had changed because she could recall how 'correct' that dress felt at the time. That sort of incident, she thought, was a good example of how many transsexuals over-feminise themselves. The problem was that some never learned.

Another sign of Miranda's changing response to the world was her conscious attempt to maintain good social links with her few friends. They had been very supportive in the year or so leading up to her operation and she saw how much joy sprang from good friendships. It was probably this positive orientation that enabled her to cope with the reunion with Jillian, who had made contact after learning of Miranda's operation. It was a sentimental reunion. Miranda's new life seemed to explain and sweep away the worst memories of their last months together years earlier. Miranda knew of course that she could never have anything other than a good friendship with Jillian, which was precisely what followed. Apart from the joy of salvaging some of the best aspects of that relationship, Miranda quietly conceded that for some time yet the issue of closer relationships with women was still too difficult to worry about. There was no urgency.

'That reunion took place almost three years ago', Miranda noted to herself. She thought about all the other significant events in the five years she had been living as a woman. The reunion was a solitary event but nevertheless a significant occasion. By contrast, she could remember many years earlier at her lowest point wondering whether she would be still around in five years. Five years was a solid test of anything. This occasion also prompted Miranda to reflect on the wider picture of transsexuals in society. She was not sure she wanted to get politically involved in any transsexual cause, but she did have some strong views about certain matters. The term 'transsexual' she felt was inappropriate because, looking back, she believed she had really not ever been anything other than a woman. Her earliest problems arose from her attempts to deny it. Above all, she was convinced that all through those years attending the clinic she had never been a 'patient'. She also thought that too many people saw the distinction between transsexuals and transvestites to be very 'black and white'. Transvestites were popularly regarded as men who dressed as women for erotic pleasure but still saw themselves as men, but the reality was many more shades of grey. Some of her contacts in the transsexual support group saw themselves as transvestites but she knew that, psychologically, they were really like her. They were consciously trying to put a gloss on their situation for a number of reasons. Some possibly believed living as women was impossible and were trying to rationalise their predicament. Others had more obvious obstacles, such as fear of threats from and rejection by family members.

Miranda's strongest resentment though was towards those who assumed that post-operative transsexuals like her would naturally experience a sexual attraction towards heterosexual men. Although she did not have a strong sex drive, she was aware she had always been sexually attracted to women. In terms of sexual attraction, she had in her own mind wanted potential partners to see her as a woman. The only change was that reassignment surgery made it possible for other women to see that. Miranda thought about the sorts of problems transsexuals face, problems such as not being able to change one's sex on a birth certificate and not being able to marry males like other women. She felt she could not take responsibility for all those problems. The future would have to be faced one step at a time. Miranda's story is clearly not finished.

A Final Comment

Many people who, in one way or another, are aware of the life situation of transsexuals will read this short excerpt and recognise patterns of events and common threads surrounding those people's lives. Some may believe they know the true identity of Miranda. Despite any similarities to any individual though, Miranda is not a real person. She is a construction from the common threads, trends and patterns running through the lives of the people who have made this study possible. It is not possible to say that Miranda is an average male to female transsexual. Not only are we unaware of the wider picture of all transsexuals, but also the notion of an average is sometimes as unhelpful as saying that the average family in Australia consists of 4.1 persons. This figure, like the cameo of Miranda, does not capture the range and extremes, although in building certain aspects of Miranda's profile, I have used some averages of my own respondents, such as the average age at which they first lived as women.

The following chapters attempt to capture those common threads, trends and patterns running through the lives of transsexuals, along with the range and extremes of their experiences.

4
The Macro Process of Becoming a Woman

'And where you are is where you are not'
T. S. Eliot

The people who made this study possible are the focus of this chapter. Interviews with the many transsexuals who cooperated in this project provided a vast amount of evidence which, when supplemented with other sources,[1] will help to answer many of the unanswered questions foreshadowed earlier. At the same time, addressing those questions will provide a means of critically evaluating the worth of the variety of approaches to transsexualism. Also, it should clarify the career of Miranda.

In light of the quantity and quality of evidence, my analysis is from both a macro and micro vantage point. I do not want to put too fine a point on these terms but by 'macro' I am referring to that level of analysis where one stands back and tries to capture the broad social patterns which apply to all transsexuals. 'Micro' is more concerned with the nature of face to face interactions involving individuals' feelings and responses. These two approaches partly overlap in that many of the micro elements in transsexuals' social experiences are patterned and aspects of broad patterns contain micro elements. The distinction is a convenient one though and can be likened to the distinction between landscape and group photography: it is a question of how far back the observer stands.

The principal insight from a macro vantage point, the focus of this chapter, is that, for transsexuals, becoming a woman is a social process. (From this point on, references to transsexuals are generally to those individuals who were the subjects in this study. Where the term involves the wider category of transsexuals, this will be made clear in the text.) It is not a process that emphasises the necessary and sufficient conditions or causes of a string of events. Rather, it is a series of stages in time akin to Kubler-Ross's (1970) stages of dying. The six stages in the process of becoming a woman are:

1 abiding anxiety
2 discovery
3 purging and delay
4 acceptance
5 surgical reassignment
6 invisibility.

Transsexuals do not necessarily experience all stages but, as with the Kubler-Ross model, they experience them in the same order. Some skip a stage and some do not go beyond the first couple of stages in the series. Also, as the horizontal zones in figure 4:1

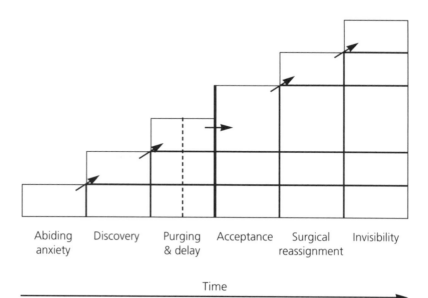

| Abiding anxiety | Discovery | Purging & delay | Acceptance | Surgical reassignment | Invisibility |

Time

Figure 4:1   *Stages in the macro process of becoming a woman*

suggest, some stages extend into and overlap with the next. Although these stages are linked serially from left to right, different locations within any stage are not necessarily points in time for any individual transsexual. Abiding anxiety, for example, *can* extend into subsequent stages, which implies that there may be those who have reached the stage of acceptance but who continue to experience anxiety, just as there are those who have no anxiety at all. At the same time though, the step-like movement across figure 4:1 indicates that with each stage something new is added. It needs to be stressed that figure 4:1 is not trying to convey the nature of any individual's experience but more the patterned nature of transsexuals' experiences as a whole.

These stages are a social process because they take place in a social context that shapes the very nature of transsexuals' experience in each stage. It is the social nature of this macro process which helps clarify some of the problems raised in chapter two, such as the question of whether gender is a social construction. What follows is a close look at transsexuals in each of the stages and the social factors that account for their similar and varied experiences in the process of becoming a woman.

Abiding Anxiety

It is difficult to be precise in the analysis of this early period in transsexuals' lives because the evidence is almost totally dependent on their memory of those events.[2] Also, it is difficult to assess to what extent the past is being constructed in terms of individuals' present circumstances. Nevertheless, it is possible to locate clear patterns among answers to simple questions that were less amenable to embellishment. Answers to questions about age at various points in the development of their transsexualism, for example, reveal some internal similarities and differences which bear on the nature of abiding anxiety.

All transsexuals in this study passed through, or are still experiencing, abiding anxiety, which is uncomfortable, and at first inexplicable feelings about sexual identity and gender. This anxiety is patterned and reveals dominant and minor themes.[3] Concerning the former, transsexuals experienced the onset of anxiety relatively early, that is, on average at age seven. It was initially relieved by cross dressing. They had a bad experience of school, characterised by teasing and bullying (see Stuart 1983). They also identified with girls rather than boys during childhood and had consulted psychiatrists before making contact with the Gender Dysphoria Clinic. Less common were the minor themes of drug use, trouble with the police, and attempted suicide.

The early anxieties of transsexuals were generally associated with the conviction of being different from other boys. The often taken for granted assumption in infancy that they would grow up to be a girl was challenged by the onset of anxiety over their maleness. The assumption of 'didn't everyone feel this way' was replaced by anxiety surrounding perceptions of the increasing significance of their genitals and what was socially expected of males. Claims that 'I should have been born a girl', 'I am the product of a biological mistake' and 'my body is not mine' were commonly heard, accompanied by feelings of 'being in limbo', 'being displaced', 'not fitting in with boys' and 'life is playing a nasty joke on me'. This anxiety is captured by one post-operative transsexual writing about her own experience and, although not interviewed for this study, she is worth quoting at length:

In those early years, my days were well filled with the business of eating, sleeping, going to school, drawing, dreaming. Probably the full significance of my problem had still to dawn on me, since I was still able, to some extent, to put it to one side. It would only get in the way when I wanted to do something that 'boys didn't do'—though there seemed to be a growing number of those. Later it became more persistent, and there were times when it was actually frightening. Those moments are the most difficult of all to describe. They would occur anywhere—at home, at school, or while I was playing. Suddenly the strangest feeling would engulf me like a wave. If I were walking along, the intensity of it would stop me in my tracks. It wasn't pain, or nausea, or giddiness, but an overwhelming sensation of uncleanness, of not belonging—to anything or anyone, family, friends, the planet, or even myself. There seemed to me *space* between me and the body I stood in, like a skeleton in a suit of armour lined with something unpleasant. I didn't fit. It was awful ... I believe every transsexual knows only too well the feeling I experienced during those awful moments of seeming to hang in space:'I am in the wrong body'. For that is the feeling (Wells 1986: 9-10, her emphasis).

These feelings of anxiety were compounded by punishment for being different. Bullying at school for being unlike the 'other boys' and/or being 'a sissy' was accompanied by feelings of rejection, loneliness and lack of confidence. Less frequently, parental disapproval of effeminate behaviour, and especially punishment from fathers, exacerbated transsexuals' inability to discuss their anxieties with their parents. In this context of abiding anxiety, it is not surprising that most transsexuals saw themselves as 'loners' in their primary school years and unable to enjoy and apply themselves to school work. One transsexual, who was interviewed for a popular women's magazine, caught most of these elements by noting that

> I knew something wasn't right when I was young, but I didn't know what it was ... I was always a sissy at school. I used to get teased all the time, even by the teachers. All the boys started to go through puberty except me. I was scared of them and used to spend all my time with the girls (*Woman's Day* 1989: 12).

One clear pattern of similarity among transsexuals is that most began cross dressing in their mother's or sister's clothes at the same time or a little after first experiencing anxiety over their sexual ambivalence. By the time they were twelve years of age, which was some two years before their average age of puberty, almost all (93 per cent) were experiencing anxiety and were cross dressing. About half recall the onset of puberty as being a difficult and stressful point in their lives. It is certainly not surprising that, given the strong theme of childhood identification with girls by wanting to be with them and to be like them, even to the extent of being jealous of them, those who found puberty difficult were those who were distressed at the appearance of body hair and a deep voice. Whatever physical resemblence they may have had to girls was disappearing with the onset of manhood.

Although transsexuals' sexual interests around the time of puberty were spread across attraction to girls, boys or neither, those who attempted relationships with girls recall experiencing anxiety over not feeling like a male, wanting to be treated as a female, and being unsuccessful in sexual intercourse. One transsexual thought her responses to girls at that time meant that she must have been a gay male. The problem was that she 'didn't feel gay'.

Generally, transsexuals carried their anxiety for at least a decade before they received their first information about transsexualism, which was, on average, around eighteen years of age. To emphasise the private and intense nature of that anxiety, it is important to acknowledge that a third were convinced they were women before they had any access to information about transsexualism. Without an adequate explanation of that conviction and not knowing that there were others who felt the same way, it is reasonable to suppose their assumptions of the idiosyncratic nature of their situation only reinforced anxiety.

Whether consultation with psychiatrists was before or after entering the next stage of the process of becoming a woman, the important point to stress is that it occurred before contact with the Gender Dysphoria Clinic. To the extent that those consultations were made after entering the stage of discovery only makes explicit the point that it did not necessarily signal the end of anxiety. As figure 4:1 attempts to convey, anxiety extended into the discovery stage.

The minor themes of drug use, trouble with the police and attempted suicide were each evident in approximately 15 per cent of transsexuals. There was some overlap of these activities but they by no means involved the same individuals. It is difficult to say much more than this about these themes in light of the sensitive nature of those activities and the difficulty for transsexuals to remember details of their past. However, they do seem to be consistent with being in a state of abiding anxiety.

The transsexuals in this study by definition have moved into at least the stage of discovery, the stage at which they are able to put a name to their feelings. I say 'by definition' because in most cases they 'know' they are transsexuals because they want a 'sex change'. Finally, and to foreshadow an issue to be taken up in the final chapter, it is not only transsexuals who experience anxiety over their sexual identity, have no knowledge of why they feel the way they do and have not sought professional help.

Discovery

Discovery of information on transsexualism was the key to most transsexuals' recognition of themselves as 'transsexuals'. Although, strictly speaking, transsexualism is not an explanation of a particular configuration of sexual identity, for transsexuals it provided a quasi-explanation of their feelings. By providing an identifiable category to which they belonged, their feelings and abiding anxiety were no longer private and idiosyncratic. Capturing this facet of discovery, one transsexual noted:

> I was glad when I discovered what I am. I knew then that what I'd been going through was not just something wrong with me.

Moreover, the medical profession's recognition of 'transsexuals' as a category attracting legitimate medical concern pointed to the possibility of surgical intervention to realise previously private fantasies of being women.

Although one-third of the transsexuals were convinced of their identity as women before they saw themselves as 'transsexuals', half discovered they were transsexual at the same time or after they first had access to information on transsexualism, which was on average around eighteen years of age. The actual nature of discovery varied from the accidental to the purposeful. Some discovered transsexualism through a process of searching. One transsexual persisted with library searches, reasoning that 'society pigeon holes everyone, therefore I must be something'. Accidental discoveries generally involved stumbling across a magazine article or a television program on transsexualism or something indirectly related, such as a story on Les Girls. In all cases, discovery took the form of individuals realising that 'this is me'. A popular magazine, quoting one transsexual, captured this accidental nature of discovery:

I lacked confidence and was always crying. I didn't know why. Then, when I was 17, I read a book about a girl who has undergone a sex change and for the first time I understood what was wrong with me (*Woman's Day* 1989: 12).

The fact that 80 per cent first desired reassignment surgery at the same time as obtaining information about transsexualism suggests that discovery was more than an intellectual event. The quasi-explanation provided by discovery pointed to surgery as a blueprint for a course of action. Desiring and acting, however, are not the same thing, a difference evident in the long gap for many between discovery and making first contact with the Gender Dysphoria Clinic. This gap ranged from one to thirty years with over half waiting more than ten years.

This variation of waiting periods also says something about the nature of abiding anxiety. For some, that waiting period was relatively short because discovery brought insight and defined a path of action. Others, for a variety of reasons, could not act on the knowledge of being transsexual, which only compounded their anxiety. The longer the delay the more vivid were the accounts of contrived male behaviour during that period. For example, some described deliberately accentuating male body language and voice. Others said they grew a beard hoping it would divert attention and prevent people 'picking up' what they 'felt just beneath the surface'. A few transsexuals admitted reluctantly trying the 'gay scene' because they did not want their, mainly, gay friends to discover their situation (see Stuart 1983: 47). Despite this variation of ploys to maintain male identity, the common theme was transsexuals' awareness of continuing stress and anxiety associated with trying to 'pass' as men but knowing that in their minds they were women. An articulate transsexual graphically expressed the nature of her continuing anxiety after discovery of her transsexualism:

Having to contrive at being a male, having to watch everything you say and to be always checking your behaviour is very stressful. The feeling is difficult to describe but it's like being a straight male who is built like a brick shithouse having to play at being a woman.

It is worth noting that, although transsexuals rarely used the term 'passing' to describe their attempts to live as women, in the situation above the term is appropriate. Passing implies deception and all transsexuals saw their contrived appearance as men as deception, which was an integral part of their anxiety. It therefore follows that transsexuals living as women cannot be described as 'passing' because, in their terms, there is no deception: they are what they see themselves to be. This issue will be addressed in the following chapter.

The waiting period of one to thirty years between discovery and making first contact with the Gender Dysphoria Clinic begs an explanation. The short period for some transsexuals indicates that discovery was soon followed by acceptance. Based on the stages in figure 4:1, these people skipped the stage I call purging and delay. A close look at this stage helps to explain the variation in the time between discovery and action.

Purging and Delay

Purging is that phase after discovery when the prospect of living as a 'woman' became a problem for transsexuals who consciously attempted to rid themselves of that sexual identity. The term 'purging' is deliberate because it is meant to convey something more active and observable than a term like denial. Kubler-Ross's (1970) depiction of 'denial', for instance, is a stage in the dying process characterised more by a person's state of mind and emotional intensity, or lack of it, than active intervention in the world. By contrast, purging is the recognisable phase transsexuals in this study entered when, in addition to denying their identity as women, they actively sought through a variety of means to conform to a male blueprint to confirm their identity as men.

Delay covers both the conscious awareness of avoiding the decision to live as a woman and the non-conscious postponement of that decision during purging. It is important to stress that this stage of 'purging and delay' is based on transsexuals in this study. The fact that almost all interviewees were attending the Gender Dysphoria Clinic means that, with a few exceptions, they had passed through purging and delay and were in the stage of acceptance. It is not possible to ascertain how many transsexuals are

socially invisible because they are locked into lengthy delays or
have 'successfully' purged themselves of their earlier identities as
women. This is an important point to which I will return.
Among the transsexuals in this study, not all delays involved purging but purging certainly represented a delay, which is why they
are treated together. This is represented in Figure 4:1 by the column with the vertical dotted line. The area to the left of the line
represents purging, whereas the whole column represents delay.

Marriage was the principal mechanism of purging. As a dominant pattern it was often accompanied by explicit masculine
activities, such as joining the armed services, heavy drinking
and/or drug taking, body building and playing men's sports. Over
half of transsexuals interviewed had been married[4] and of those
nearly two-thirds had children. With or without children, their
accounts of marriage generally acknowledged their awareness that
the decision to marry was also a decision to 'sort out' the mind
and to 'prove once and for all' that by marrying a woman one
was a 'man', especially when children ensued. Of course, this is
not to deny that many of those transsexuals had genuinely close
relationships with their partners and subsequently had what they
freely admit were worthwhile marriages. The fact that those marriages did not last, however, prompts a closer look at transsexuals'
attempts to purge themselves of their identities as women. This is
also important if only to preclude transsexualism as an elaborate
post hoc justification of a failed marriage.[5]

Although it is not possible to be absolutely certain, most transsexuals' marriages appear as if they could never have worked. At
one extreme, tensions in those relationships began immediately
after marriage. A fifth of married transsexuals confessed their
history of cross dressing to their wives within months of marrying
and subsequently were dressing as women in front of their wives
in the privacy of their home. This pattern also is evident among a
handful of cases found in analysis of the files of post-operative
transsexuals. On a few occasions I noted evidence of wives
attending for interviews with psychologists and psychiatrists and
commenting that they were not really married to a man. One
noted that her husband responded to her 'as a sister'. Another felt
that her marriage was more like 'a relationship with a lesbian'.

All the married transsexuals described some sort of difficulty in
their sexual relationships with their wives. For some, sexual

intercourse ceased a few years after marriage, that is, after their children were born. Others confessed to infrequent intercourse that was only possible by fantasising about being the female partner and being penetrated. A few described bitter emotional incidents associated with attempts to have sexual intercourse while cross dressed.

Therefore, it is reasonably clear that married transsexuals' transsexualism was not a last minute justification of a failed marriage but, instead, a key factor in that failure. What is less clear is whether transsexuals actually approached their marriages with the conscious aim of 'straightening out' their confused sexual identities. Their accounts of marriage certainly reveal purging as a dominant theme but, as we all see the past largely in terms of our current vantage point, their telling the truth or constructing their past attitudes is not the issue. This is simply because we really have no way of knowing whether they are accurate. The issue then is not whether at the time of marriage they necessarily thought they were purging themselves of their identities as women, but whether *now* they genuinely interpret their marriages as purging. Most transsexuals, however, stressed they *were* conscious of marrying so they could be rid of their confused gender identity. One, who was post-operative, offered the comment, as if recalling a very recent event:

> I got married at least partly to stop people treating me as a pretty boy and partly so that I could get rid of my confusion about my gender.

Others were convinced of their actual feelings at the time of marriage because they could provide a detailed history of a variety of other purging activities. The few who joined the services openly accounted for that decision as one post-operative transsexual expressed it:

> I tried to suppress the feelings [of wanting to be a woman], so I made a courageous effort to conform as a man, so much so I joined the navy.

Purging also extended to a range of other strategies. These included heavy drinking; drug use in a male subculture, where drugs meant being accepted by men as 'a man' thus providing 'a mask for being an oddity'; having extramarital affairs; body building; playing men's sports; and having, as one transsexual put it, 'an affair with two girls to prove I was no different from any other man'. Frequently, I read in transsexuals' files comments by professionals, such as 'he always wanted to be a girl but he has tried to deny it by playing football'. For those transsexuals who tried in different ways to convince themselves they were not women, their attempts at purging were unsuccessful and represented variable delays of acceptance.

Unsuccessful purging was accompanied by varying levels of anxiety. At one extreme, a few transsexuals reflected on their recognition that they had not resolved their gender confusion through marriage by calmly noting that that period in their lives was more tense than usual. Commenting on how she felt emotionally, one transsexual just noted 'it was a difficult time'. At another extreme, other transsexuals were more graphic, describing a daily cycle of recurring and increasing tension over their lack of success at being 'a married man'. A middle aged, pre-operative transsexual described the last decade of her marriage as 'an attempt to dismiss the idea of ever being a woman [but] the doubts kept returning'.

All purging involved delay in accepting that living as a woman was the only way to deal with confusion of sexual identity. Not all delay, however, involved purging. For a large minority of transsexuals, especially, but not exclusively, the younger and unmarried ones, there was no evidence of attempts to purge their desire to live as women. Although the desire was constant, the delay stemmed from perceived obstacles in the social realm rather than the vain attempt at living as men. Of course, those transsexuals who pursued the latter course, and later reached the point of recognising that they could not rid themselves of the desire to live as women, were in the same position as the former category when they could not immediately act on those desires.

The obstacles to realising the desire to be a woman were real to transsexuals. 'One may know what one is but doing something about it is another matter' was the view of one pre-operative transsexual who captured the sentiments of most others.

Obstacles were not idiosyncratic to individuals but form patterns which all transsexuals experienced or were still experiencing to a greater or lesser extent. Those patterns were in the contexts of family, work and religion and also included the view of the self.

The view of the physical self

The view of the physical self, or just 'self', is the way any transsexual sees herself physically as a woman vis-a-vis being a biological male. It is not a complex or sophisticated concept that is meant to incorporate psychological dimensions, such as self-understanding and self-esteem, although those notions cannot be excluded. It was illustrated by a middle aged, pre-operative transsexual who began by asking me what I thought of her general appearance as a woman. She went on to add:

> I often stand in front of a mirror and wonder whether I'm kidding myself. I have to admit that the body is a bit over the hill. When you're in your forties you've got a lot more to contend with. There's the problem of this [referring to facial hair] ... as well as unlearning to be a male.

The more micro aspects of this sentiment will be dealt with in the following chapter, for the body and especially particular parts of it assume considerable importance in the process of becoming a woman. What is important at this point is that transsexuals' views of themselves varied and that variation was associated with delay.

Age, not surprisingly, is the most obvious predictor of the view of the self. The youngest transsexuals, especially those in their late teens, were more confident in presenting as women largely because their view of themselves met no contradictions. Their bodies resembled those of a biological female, especially if they had been taking female hormones, and they had not known anything different. They had never lived as men. It is important to stress that this resemblance goes beyond mere body shape. Among the younger transsexuals, this resemblance was to an array of body characteristics not related to any particular individual female but more to a conventional image of feminine beauty. The more their own characteristics, especially height, weight, skin texture, hair, breast size and nose shape, conformed to that image, the more positive was their view of self. Although no one explicitly saw the well-known British transsexual Caroline Cossey, who is pictured opposite, as the standard by which they should measure their appearance, their preferences for medium height, a slim figure, soft skin, long hair, at least average breast size, a petite nose and no obvious 'adam's apple' were thematic.

By contrast, older, but not necessarily the oldest, transsexuals had lived as men and in many cases were fathers. Consequently, they had more reservations about how they saw themselves as women. Those reservations, for example, surrounded being a stern devil's advocate of their own appearance when standing in front of a mirror. The important theme though is that their confidence and doubts were related to the same broad image of feminine beauty found among younger transsexuals.[6] With the importance of this image of femininity in mind, it is more than coincidental that tall, heavy men with considerable body hair are under-represented among those transsexuals interviewed. One could speculate that in the wider society there are many tall, heavy male to female transsexuals and that their individual view of self as a woman is negative because of its lack of correspondence with a certain image of femininity. The consequence is that they remain socially invisible and never seek professional assistance.

A small minority of older transsexuals I interviewed had no reservations about how they saw themselves as women. Largely because of their age and their own perceptions that they could never conform to that image of feminine beauty, they saw being a woman as constituted by more than appearances. One actually used terms such as 'dowdy' and 'ordinary' to describe herself, admitting that she did not try to look 'beautiful' but deliberately dressed 'down market' so that she did not 'make a fool' of herself.

Regardless of whether transsexuals had confidence or doubts, or whether they attempted to conform to a certain image of feminine beauty or not, their view of the self can be measured by its distance from that shared image of feminine beauty. This pattern is all the more profound when the experiences of transsexuals who have attempted to maintain a 'unisex' appearance are examined. This small minority described their earlier attempts at looking like neither a man nor a woman because they did not wish to conform to stereotyped, gendered appearances. All found, however, that a unisex appearance was not possible in a gendered or sexed world, which is consistent with Foucault's

Caroline Cossey, the well-known British transsexual, is a professional model and has appeared in films. She is also an author, having recently written her autobiography (see References).

(1980: vii) observation that modern western societies have responded 'in the affirmative' to the question '[D]o we *truly* need a *true* sex?' Apart from the many situations in which sex or gender needs to be declared, such as applying for a driver's licence, there were too many obstacles at the day to day level, for example, being challenged when entering a public toilet and potential lovers not being sure whether they were with an effeminate man or a masculine woman. One post-operative transsexual conveyed some of her difficulty with an earlier attempt at an androgynous lifestyle:

> the ambiguity in the eyes of others was difficult to bear. I felt I needed to have certainty, not only in my own mind, but also in the mind of the public.

Another transsexual summed up the frustration of her unisex phase with the comment, 'I found I couldn't go forward and I couldn't go back [to living as a man]'.

Family

The family, which includes wives, children and parents, was for most transsexuals both a source of support and the main reason for delay in moving to the next stage. For married transsexuals, although the line between purging and recognition of the need to do something about living full time as a woman was a fine one, when it did occur it was generally followed by delay associated with family ties.

Children were the principal reason for transsexuals' delaying their moving on to the acceptance stage. Accounts of their reasons and feelings at that time revolved around the need to delay disruption to family life. This delay was for a number of often overlapping reasons that included feelings of responsibility as a father, fear of losing contact with children and the need to give them time to reach an age of independence. Moreover, there were emotional bonds with children, and often with wives, that in themselves were enjoyable and not easy to turn away from. There were also more indirect reasons. Children were costly to support, which meant important stepping stones to living as a woman, such as paying off the house, were just that much further away. There was also the knowledge that to the outside world being a father represented security in that it camouflaged any hint of not being what one appeared to be.

Consistent with the picture during the purging phase, married transsexuals' accounts of delay during those years preceding acceptance appeared to be more than *post hoc* justifications of their decisions to live as women. There was clear evidence of conscious, rational delaying strategies in the comments of one pre-operative, middle aged transsexual, who spoke of her 'long range planning' towards living as a woman full time. She devised a 'timetable' of the goals she hoped to achieve by certain dates, such as paying off the house, completing electrolysis for facial hair removal, and accumulating a specific amount of capital. Other transsexuals described actually making preliminary contact with the Gender Dysphoria Clinic but holding off from making appointments until family matters were 'sorted out'.

Parents were a source of delay for two identifiable reasons. The first concerned the nature of emotional ties with family. For a married transsexual, parents and a wife's parents together represented a network. Just as that network could provide support, it was also capable of exerting pressure to achieve conformity. Around half the transsexuals with children described some equivocation about acting on their transsexuality because of the fear of being shunned and because of the doubts and guilt feelings raised by this sort of family network. Younger transsexuals generally admitted to their needing parental support before they could do anything about their transsexuality. To the extent that they lacked that support, the family was a source of delay. Only 40 per cent of all transsexuals claimed they had general support, with around 15 per cent receiving no support and a similar proportion having mother's support only. The threat of physical violence was the second reason parents were a source of delay. Whether married or not, a few transsexuals related stories of family intimidation that led to fear, anxiety and lack of conviction in seeking professional assistance. One pre-operative transsexual, for example, graphically described her father putting a shotgun to her head and threatening to use it if ever she went ahead with reassignment surgery. Another described how repeated physical threats from her family forced her to 'leave town'.

Work

Three interrelated aspects of transsexuals' world of work affected delay in the stage of purging and delay. They were the degree of friendship and support, the perceived gendered nature of the job, and income. For most people in the workforce work is a source of friendship and support. Similar to the family situation, in the transition to living as a woman, the degree of support in the workplace was associated with the length of delay. There were, not surprisingly, the same sort of doubts which were evident in the family context, such as 'will they understand?' and 'will they reject me?' But here delay sprang from more than uncertainty surrounding these questions.

Regardless of the type of work, those transsexuals in the workforce faced a problem. In situations where other staff had no idea of their transsexuality, each was aware that 'he' was regarded by others in the workplace as just another male colleague. Moreover, effective work practices and informal friendships existed largely because of being seen as a male. Given the imperative nature of the need to live as a woman, however, the problem was how could one become a convincing female overnight? A pre-operative transsexual who agonised about the transition to being a woman at work captured this difficulty:

> It's not just a matter of leaving work on Friday night as [man's name] and turning up on Monday as [woman's name]. It's not as if you can just shave off your beard and come in the next day with a smooth complexion. Electrolysis takes time. But I'm not sure I want to be into that while I'm still just another bloke at work. I don't want them asking questions. So how do you cross over? I have to do it but I couldn't cope with being seen as a guy in a dress ... I'd have no support.

The actual transition to being a woman in the workplace will be dealt with in the examination of the stage of acceptance. Generally though, the extent of workplace support and transsexuals' positive experiences of the transition to being a woman in that situation provided a rough measure of their equivocation and, therefore, delay preceding it.

The perceived gendered nature of transsexuals' jobs delayed the transition to being a woman in the workplace. Those transsexuals who were working as men in male dominated blue collar jobs believed that they could not work as women in the same situation and needed to find alternative employment if they were going to make the transition. This situation represented a delay in relation to those in white collar, mixed gendered jobs, not just because of the need to find a new job and 'retool', but also because it often involved moving from one city to another.

Although, as we will see in the next stage, being in a white collar job was no guarantee of workplace support, it was nevertheless possible to contemplate making the transition at work, because certain jobs in computing, clerical work and teaching, for example, were not associated with or dominated by either gender. Incidentally, those few transsexuals who were self-employed at the time of making the transition were in white collar jobs that were not dominated by one gender. Any delay in their transition did not stem from workplace colleagues but from anticipated reactions of clients, who in each case seem to have been supportive.

By contrast, those in blue collar jobs had difficulty contemplating working as women in the same jobs. In accounting for why they decided to change jobs, those transsexuals who left blue collar work stressed the nature of the job itself as the reason rather than the hostile response they would have received from their colleagues. In other words, they saw blue collar manual work as not appropriate for women. Looking back, a post-operative transsexual, who is now in professional work, captured this gendered orientation of her previous job:

> I worked in a factory before I made the decision about reassignment. It was hot and dirty, you would end up covered in grease by the end of the day ... well, it was not possible to continue in that job if I was going to live as a woman. I know I was good at it but it was so dirty.

Income also affected delay in making the decision to live as a woman and, as the subsequent stages demonstrate, it continues to affect the process of becoming a woman. This was most evident among the relatively high proportion of unemployed transsexuals who repeatedly pointed to the cost of buying women's clothes, finding their own place to live, and/or the prospect of having to pay for medical expenses. As they saw the situation, lack of money only extended the time they would have to wait before they could obtain reassignment surgery. Admittedly, delay for most unemployed transsexuals had extended into the acceptance stage. However, among the few unemployed who had not made the transition to living as women, poverty was their explanation for not doing so.

Religion

For only four transsexuals was religious belief an obvious factor in delaying their acceptance of the need to live as women. Similar to the other factors above, it is difficult to measure the precise effect of those transsexuals' strong religious beliefs on their transition. Even as a researcher, however, I could not fail to see the torment and anxiety they experienced, or were still experiencing, as they approached the biggest decision of their lives. For the two post-operative transsexuals who had made that decision, their accounts of their earlier torment and indecision were remarkably consistent with the visible distress of the other two, whose religious convictions were heightening their indecisiveness in different ways. For one, a profound sense of guilt was an obstacle to making the decision to live as a woman. For the other, who had made that decision, it was reassignment surgery that was precarious in light of her religious convictions. This was evident in her question to me: 'Creation is so perfect ... isn't surgery a crime against God?'

In all four cases, religious commitment has been a source of strength and the source of self-doubt and delay. What is significant is that despite that self-doubt and delay, three of those four people are now living as women. The other one wondered how many transsexuals never become visible and never live as women because their religious convictions help tilt them in another direction.

Purging and delay as the 'end of the road'

Of course, in speculating about invisibility, it is not only religious convictions which may contribute to transsexuals never going beyond the stage of purging and delay. Speculate is the appropriate term here because, whether transsexuals successfully 'purge' themselves of their gender confusion or just simply remain silent about it and live in a perpetual state of delay as men, we would never be aware of it. Although the former category is virtually unknowable by definition, there is indirect evidence of transsexuals who, consciously, would like to live as women but are locked into a perpetual state of delay as men.

This indirect evidence includes transsexuals' views of transvestites, which generally suggests that transvestites are not always what they appear. Although the textbook definition of transvestites holds that they are generally heterosexual men who gain sexual pleasure from dressing and being seen as women, the boundary with transsexuals is not that clear. Several transsexuals related stories about transvestites they knew through the Seahorse Club and the Elaine Barry Foundation. The notable theme, albeit a minor one, was that some of those transvestites were 'really' transsexuals. When I pursued this claim by asking how they knew, they pointed to, so-called, transvestites' envy of transsexuals being able to live full time as women and be on female hormones. Given that those transsexuals placed a great deal of significance on the act of 'going onto hormones' as the key to the distinction between transsexuals and transvestites ('TSs and TVs'), envy may have been an important discriminator.

'Transsexuals in hiding' and 'weekend transsexuals', as some transsexuals described those 'not so certain' transvestites, may use the popular definition of transvestite as a useful ploy in coping with not being able to live as women. They deliberately use the language surrounding the popular understanding of transvestite when among other transvestites because it gives legitimacy to their observable behaviour and, possibly, provides some sort of coping strategy for themselves.[7] Admittedly, this is speculative but one post-operative transsexual told me of a 'transvestite' who she believed was a transsexual. This person was also once a member of the Seahorse Club and used the opportunity to dress as a woman as a way of acting out 'his' inner feelings of wanting to live as a woman. 'He' was not able to for several reasons, principally because 'he' was married with children, successful in business and his wife's overseas extended family 'would not rest' if 'he' ever left her to live as a woman.

This social invisibility of transsexuals is not confined to living part time as a transvestite. Following feature articles in *The Age* and the *Sydney Morning Herald* about this study,[8] I received several letters and telephone calls, some anonymous, from people who told me of their frustrated, long term desire to live as women. Most of these people were transsexuals now living as women. Two were not. They were living as men but had always wanted to be women and live as women. As middle aged men, they were aware that when they should 'have done something about it' little was known, there were few supports, and public understanding was non-existent. In the meantime, they married and had children. It was then too late. One of those men wanted to discuss his situation with me personally. When we met he told me that, apart from his wife, I was the only person who knew of his past and true feelings. During that discussion I was consciously aware of asking myself: how many other men are there who have had similar experiences?

A final indirect indication of transsexuals' social invisibility is the under-representation of certain migrant categories among transsexuals I have interviewed but also among those post-operative transsexuals who have been associated with the Gender Dysphoria Clinic. Given that transsexualism has a long history and exists in all societies,[9] the question arises: where are the Italians, Greeks and people from the former Yugoslavia? These categories are mentioned only because Australia has received large numbers of migrants from those countries and, statistically, if transsexuals were equally distributed in all societies, one could expect to see a certain proportion among the two hundred-odd post-operative transsexuals who have passed through the program. Males from the countries above constitute 3.5 per cent of all males in Australia whereas those from all non-English-speaking countries represent 13.24 per cent.[10] This means that if transsexuals were equally distributed in those national categories and were equally visible, one would expect to find around two born in Italy, Greece or the former Yugoslavia and about seven from other non-English-speaking countries among the transsexuals I interviewed. Applying this projection to those post-operative transsexuals who have been through the program, there should be about seven from those three countries and twenty-seven from other non-English-speaking countries. I interviewed no one who was born in Italy, Greece or the former Yugoslavia and only two migrants from other non-English-speaking countries. Based on my analysis of files of almost two hundred post-operative transsexuals, there were only nine who were born in non-English-speaking countries.

This picture is only indirect evidence of invisible transsexuals. It is indirect because under-representation of certain migrant categories among transsexuals who are currently associated, or have completed their association, with the Gender Dysphoria Clinic does not mean that the number of invisible transsexuals is automatically calculable. It could be that there is something about being Australian born and English speaking that is strongly associated with being transsexual and the converse for non-English-speaking migrants. I stress the 'could be' because if there is something distinctive about being Australian born that is associated with being a visible transsexual, then it is not apparent. The more likely explanation is that there is something distinctive about coming from a non-English-speaking country that prevents transsexuals from ever becoming visible and thus a 'statistic'. That factor is possibly strong family ties, often involving traditional notions of honour and face, which largely hold members to strong patterns of conformity. It is difficult to say what the picture is among their Australian born children.

Acceptance

The stage of acceptance begins when a transsexual finally acknowledges that living as a woman is the only way to cope with gender confusion and sets in train the process of doing so, specifically, seeking a referral to the Gender Dysphoria Clinic. All transsexuals interviewed at the Clinic had, by definition, reached at least the beginning of acceptance. Illustrating the idea of a broad process of becoming a woman, they were not all living as women at the time of interview. Just over 40 per cent were still living as men at that time.

As acceptance implies, the transsexuals were aware of their own identities and what they wanted from the Clinic by the time of their first visit. Two dominant trends were revealing in support of this claim. First, two-thirds of the transsexuals presented for their first visit as women and of those one-third were not living full time as women. Second, not only among the people I interviewed but also based on the files of post-operative transsexuals, their reason for contacting the Clinic was for surgical reassignment. There was no evidence of anyone presenting with inexplicable anxiety, that is, asking the question 'Doctor, why am I feeling this way and what can you do?' The following excerpt from a transsexual's letter of introduction was typical of their general level of self-understanding and what they expected from the Clinic:

> I am a transsexual and have been taking female hormones for years. I would like to make an appointment at your earliest convenience to discuss the possibility of a male to female sex change operation.

Although 17 per cent of transsexuals had been on hormones for five years or more by the time of their first visit, the dominant trend (56 per cent) was that transsexuals began taking female hormones, made their first visit to the Clinic, and started living permanently as women all within a two year period. Given that a little over 40 per cent were still living as men at the time of their first visit and that around 8 per cent had lived as women for five or more years before that, the dominant trend is emphasised by the observation that their average age on the first visit to the Clinic and living full time as a woman were both thirty-one, with twenty-eight being the average age for beginning female hormones.

Acceptance can be a lengthy stage and certainly involves more than seeking a referral to the Gender Dysphoria Clinic. Before they are eligible for reassignment surgery, transsexuals must live for at least two years as women and maintain regular contact with a variety of Clinic staff. During that period, which is still current for many of the transsexuals, certain patterned responses were evident.

Gate keeping and game playing

Gate keeping and game playing are related notions which deal with one important aspect of the relationship between trans-sexuals and the Gender Dysphoria Clinic. Gate keeping is the patterned perception among transsexuals that the Clinic controls their access to surgery. The consequence of this perception for some is that they feel they must present themselves so as to conform to an image Clinic staff consider appropriate. 'Appropriate' characterises those responses and behaviour which are most conducive to gaining a recommendation for surgery. The other side of the coin is game playing, which is the contrived and artificial behaviour Clinic staff perceive among transsexuals, who behave that way because of their gate keeper image of the Clinic. Hence, gate keeping and game playing are interlinked and are an important dimension of the acceptance stage because, for most transsexuals, they characterise the path to the next stage of surgical reassignment.

The gate keeper role of the Clinic was a dominant image among transsexuals but it surfaced in a number of ways. At one extreme, a minority had a neutral image of the Clinic as gate keeper. By 'neutral' I mean transsexuals accepted the Clinic as playing a necessary and legitimate role in their careers, especially concerning being recommended for reassignment surgery. This image acknowledged the Clinic as the only one of its kind in Australia and certainly in Victoria. Although surgery can be obtained in other states with the support of two psychiatrists' assessments, the Clinic's integrated and systematic approach makes it possible for many transsexuals to make a smooth transition to living as women and proceed to surgery which, many have claimed, they would not do if they lived in other states. Emphasising the necessary role the Clinic has played in their lives, this minority acknowledged that they would have visited the Clinic years earlier had they known of its existence.

By contrast, there was a politicised image of the Clinic as gate keeper. An equally small minority of transsexuals viewed themselves as clients in relation to the Clinic as a service provider. They believed that if they were paying large sums of money for psychological testing and surgery, then they should have a say in the important decisions rather than the Clinic having all the control.[11] One transsexual, for example, who was pre-operative at the time, regarded the Clinic as 'oppressive' in terms of the extremely narrow image of suitable candidates for surgery that it 'imposed on clients'. That 'narrow image' involved the 'rigid distinction the Clinic saw between transvestites and transsexuals' and its unsubstantiated assumptions about the existence of 'true transsexuals' and 'the percentage of transsexuals who are lesbians'. By controlling access to surgery, the Clinic extracted compliance and conformity from transsexuals on the program. This same transsexual added that the Clinic did not accept the responsibility which went with the power, citing transsexuals having to sign a form absolving staff of any responsibility for negative consequences following surgery. Another pre-operative transsexual echoed the same sentiment, suggesting that the Clinic was 'too tough' in reviewing suitable cases for surgery. She added that the Clinic's approach was 'unimaginative' because candidates themselves played no role in their own paths to reassignment surgery.

The most prominent image of the gate keeper role was transsexuals' mild resentment at having to conform to a pattern of behaviour the Clinic regarded as indicative of good candidates for surgery. A post-operative transsexual, who had had reassignment surgery many years earlier, believed the Clinic was 'naive' about the world of the transsexual and doubted their ability to discriminate between good and poor candidates. She thought they had a narrow view which sometimes led to the wrong people having surgery. It also necessarily led to game playing by transsexuals who were afraid to declare their true feelings and behaviour. Her advice to other transsexuals was not to say anything about 'lesbianism, feminism or anal sex' because those activities put one's future surgery 'under a cloud'. Generally, this moderately negative perception of the Clinic corresponds with Harding's (1986: 115) comment on transsexuals' hostility towards the team and King's (1981: 183) view that transsexuals had an unpleasant experience of similar clinics in the UK.

Turning to the staff of the Clinic, they are aware that much of what they see and hear among transsexuals is game playing. Apart from what I was told, I frequently saw in the Clinic's files explicit references to contrived behaviour. One psychiatrist, for instance, provided a reasonably typical comment on a transsexual's game playing by noting that 'her story is somewhat rehearsed'. Another psychiatrist, in making a more general observation, noted that all transsexuals are wary and want to do well on tests, after all a lot really depends on having given the 'right answer'.

Similarly, a psychological test report noted that another transsexual was

defensive in testing but [that is] not unusual where the motivation for testing is solely to obtain gender reassignment.

Other comments in those files included references to candidates 'deliberately adopting a stereotypical female role' and 'constructing stereotypical sexual fantasies'.

The latter comment is borne out by an analysis of responses to a standard questionnaire administered by one of the psychiatrists to most transsexuals I interviewed. In response to a question about their fantasised sexual goal, almost all responded that they fantasised being a woman with a vagina and having sex with a heterosexual man. From my interviews with those same people, however, and based on information, in some cases, from their friends, the overwhelmingly heterosexual pattern[12] was more apparent than real or, in other words, game playing. Based on my assessment, which was often informed by direct admission by transsexuals themselves, just under half (47 per cent) could be considered to practise what they claimed to fantasise about.[13] Almost a third (31 per cent) were clearly lesbian in their sexual orientation and about one-fifth (22 per cent) asexual, although admittedly, the latter designation is difficult to apply. Based on overseas researchers' comments about a 'heterosexual bias' in medical circles, transsexuals' perception of the need to 'play the game', especially those with a lesbian orientation, could at least be an informed perception, albeit, as I suggest below, an inaccurate one regarding the Clinic (see Hausman 1992: 293; Bolin 1987b).

I should point out that my application of these labels concerning sexual orientation was conservative. I did not rely on the actual existence of a sexual relationship but categorised someone heterosexual or lesbian even if they said they would like some day to be involved in a relationship with a man or another woman.

On the other hand, those who were categorised asexual typically responded that they were 'not attracted to either men or women', that they were 'not interested in sex at all' and that their 'sex drive was just about non-existent ... it's always been that way'.[14]

I have two comments on the gate keeper–game playing picture. The first is that many transsexuals place far too much significance on the need to conform to the imagined, ideal candidate. Perseverance and consistency appear to be more important in leading to a recommendation for reassignment surgery than conformity to some moral standard. In the files of post-operative transsexuals going back to the 1970s, there are numerous instances of transsexuals being recommended for surgery even though members of the Clinic previously had expressed concerns about their suitability. This presents a less severe picture of the Clinic's gate keeper role.

Notwithstanding this qualification, the role of the Clinic as gate keeper, even beyond the neutral sense, is unavoidable. To the extent that reassignment surgery can only be performed by doctors in hospitals and that public funds are implicated, medical professionals believe that the politics of the situation demand erring on the side of caution in recommending candidates for surgery. Surgery is not recommended for transsexuals with severe mental illness, certainly for psychiatric reasons but also, presumably, because of the legal implications of any unpredictable consequences. Also, cautious screening is adopted to locate those transsexuals who, later, are likely to have second thoughts about the desirability of their 'new body' and want their surgery reversed. A few rare cases of requests for 'reversals' exist in the files of the Clinic and one can only speculate about the political consequences of large numbers of those transsexuals going public with complaints about a Clinic recommending 'drastic, irreversible surgery'!

My second comment concerns the significance of transsexuals' game playing in their relations with Clinic staff. If one were to assume that only transsexuals indulge in this sort of game playing in the clinical arena, then there may be something important about the activities described above. Given transsexuals in this study appear to be no different from other transsexuals[15] and their game playing, King suggests that there is nothing unusual about interviewees' game playing because it is a feature of medicine in general. King criticises Billings and Urban (1982) and Sagarin (1978) who see transsexuals 'conning' their doctors in the hope of getting reassignment surgery. He counters by saying that, concerning

> the interactions between doctors and transsexuals, they [for instance, Sagarin and Billings and Urban] are pointing to some-thing peculiar and disreputable about the phenomenon. However it is possible to counter-argue that they are merely describing processes that have long been recognised as pertain-ing to medicine in general ... Just as the ethnomethodologist ... sees the transsexual's behaviour as an illustration of how everybody 'does' gender, we can see 'transsexualism' as an illustration of how illness generally is 'done' (King 1993: 187).

Finally, the perception of the Clinic as gate keeper was not spread evenly but was more closely associated with those transsex-uals who strongly desired reassignment surgery. In turn, there was a relationship between the intensity of transsexuals' desire for surgery and their age and, to a lesser extent, their occupational background. Younger transsexuals—that is, between twenty-one and thirty-three[16]—were generally more intense about wanting surgery and more vocal about the Clinic's gate keeper role. Older transsexuals—that is, thirty-four to fifty-four, especially those who were in white collar professional occupations—were less concerned about accelerating the date for surgery.

Support groups

Almost half of the transsexuals in this study admitted to some association with one or more support groups. In turn, about half of those had been or were members of Transition, an association that had around twelve members in 1993 and has since disbanded. A smaller number belonged to the Elaine Barry Foundation or the Seahorse Club. An even smaller number once were associated with the Transsexual Liberation Front, a more marginal group, and the Victorian Transsexual Coalition that was founded in the late 1970s but no longer exists. A new group called the Victorian Transsexual Support Association was formed in early 1994. Its founding members saw it initially having a 'reformist' role, although later the support role would be developed.

The association Transition was viewed positively by those who had been members. One prominent member spoke of the role Transition played for transsexuals, who 'come and go' depending on their need for contact. At that time, she saw three types of person belonging to the group. There were lonely people, power seekers, and those who genuinely wanted to help other transsexuals. Generally speaking though, she felt that regardless of the sort of person, the 'further down the track' transsexuals go, the less support groups are necessary.

This same sentiment was echoed by members of the other groups. Possibly as part of their decreasing need for membership, they were critical of the Elaine Barry Foundation and the Seahorse Club. All who were members had isolated complaints such as the groups' concern for increasing the number of members rather than caring for them and members' preoccupation with reaching the post-operative stage, especially at the Seahorse Club. Common to all members of both groups was the complaint that they were really clubs for transvestites rather than transsexuals. One ex-member of the Seahorse Club saw it as just a place where 'men dressed as women talked about football'.

It is difficult to say why other people chose not to belong to support groups. The retort from one pre-operative transsexual that 'I don't want to join a support group for transsexuals because I'm not a transsexual, I'm a woman' may be a common sentiment. Whatever support these groups provided, however, it appears it was needed for a limited time. Some of the benefits though continued after leaving, such as ex-members staying in touch with each other and other transsexuals. Some interviewees could list up to twenty-five other transsexuals they knew through networks originating from support groups.

The transition at work

Acceptance also involved acknowledging being a woman in other important settings such as the workplace. How did those 69 per cent of transsexuals in the workforce[17] make the transition? Four strategies were clear but care should be taken in viewing them as strong trends or patterns. Good evidence on the workplace was difficult to obtain because only two or three people characterised each strategy. The strategies are worth spelling out though because they represent some striking contrasts in terms of varying acceptance in the workplace and indirectly clarify the earlier stage of delay. The strategies are:

1 toughing it out
2 changing jobs
3 dropping hints
4 using an intermediary.

Toughing it out involved transsexuals simply announcing at work that from a particular date they would assume full time the identity of a woman. They would also be known by the new name they had legally adopted and expected work colleagues to acknowledge this change of identity. In each case the announcement was by means of a letter sent to all colleagues. There was minimal delay, with the transition occurring over a weekend and, it appears, with little forewarning. The success of this strategy seems to have been related to support from colleagues both before and after the transition rather than the type of job the person was employed in. For example, one transsexual, who worked in a warehouse as a fork lift driver, thought that she had made the transition successfully. She added that

> the men who worked there were pretty rough and they called me by my new name but would still say 'he did this' and 'he did that'. But my mates in the warehouse were behind me. They just told me not to worry and that they would take care of me. They made it known to others that that sort of thing was not on. They did look after me.

By contrast, another transsexual, who worked in a professional position, had a difficult transition. After declaring her intention to live as a woman, her job was redefined so that, she believed, she would have less exposure to the public. Further, her situation was made more difficult by colleagues raising problems about her altered identity, such as using the female toilets. The perceived lack of support from the workplace in this person's case, although extending into the acceptance stage, indicates one of the main reasons for equivocation and, therefore, delay before transition.

Changing jobs was probably the easiest strategy because it meant that fellow workers did not witness the transition of a colleague from male to female. Most transsexuals who were students adopted this strategy, with a few changing their city of residence at the same time. Their new work colleagues assumed they were working with a woman whose gender they took for granted. The significance of this taken for grantedness will be discussed in the following chapter.

The few transsexuals who dropped hints of their transsexuality found that over time they had alerted their colleagues to an imminent change. Strategies included wearing an earring in each ear; growing long fingernails; and deliberately leaving behind traces of nail polish and eye make up. The transsexuals adopting this strategy were tentative about revealing their desire to live and work as women and seemed to hope that their colleagues would actually ask them when they were going to 'come out'. One of those who had not made the transition said that she was afraid of telling people at work and had been dropping hints for months. She knew she soon had to make an announcement and hoped that when she finally did it would be low keyed. She was expecting her colleagues 'to say something like, "we wondered when you'd get around to telling us what we've known for some time"'.

Use of an intermediary occurred in three cases in workplaces with a large number of employees. In each case, during the transsexual's extended holiday away from work, a colleague who was well-known, such as a counsellor, informed staff of the imminent transition. This involved writing letters to all staff and, in one case, addressing them on the factual picture of transsexualism. Later those three transsexuals had an unexpectedly smooth experience of assuming the identity of women at work. In this sort of situation, however, it is difficult to say what was influencing what. The presence of an intermediary may have been saying something more about the crucial role of support in the workplace rather than the effectiveness of an intermediary *per se*.

When the four self-employed transsexuals made their transition their experiences were not unlike those above. Two told clients in the same way as those employed transsexuals who 'toughed it out' at the workplace. Clients accepted their decision to change their gender, acknowledging that that was a private matter and not important in the world of business. The other two, who became self-employed after their transition, had not told their clients and have had the same experience as those transsexuals who changed jobs.

Finally, it is worth noting the experiences of the relatively large proportion of transsexuals who were unemployed. For those who could not find work and those who felt they needed to change their type of work, having an income was crucial in the decision to live full time as women. Therefore, factors affecting the gaining of income impinge on transsexuals' experience of the acceptance stage. A minority of the unemployed had taken retraining courses under the Commonwealth Rehabilitation Scheme but it was the perception of the more recent interviewees that that sort of retraining was no longer available. Generally, transsexuals seeking benefits through government agencies, particularly the Department of Social Security, have not had a positive experience in dealing with both staff and management who 'ridiculed' and 'discriminated' against transsexuals.

Surgical Reassignment

Notwithstanding the somewhat inaccurate perception many transsexuals had of the Clinic as a harsh gate keeper, it is still the case that it controls access to surgery in terms of who is recommended and how soon after the mandatory two year period of living as women. Therefore factors which influence the Clinic's view of the suitability of any candidate for surgery are important to consider because, at worst, they may lead to a refusal to undertake reassignment surgery and, at best, may result in a reduction of the mandatory two year waiting period.[18] In between those extremes, various factors influence the length of time transsexuals need to wait for surgery after that two year period.

Lack of money is one of the obvious factors influencing the timing of surgery. Approved candidates who are not able to pay private hospital fees often have to wait some time because of the limited public funds available for reassignment surgery. Delay can be compounded in situations where a transsexual's poverty is associated with lack of education, long term unemployment, little motivation, depression and even poor personal hygiene. I am aware of a few cases where the Clinic saw this sort of situation as a contraindication of surgery, which was postponed until those individuals' circumstances improved.

The Clinic has also extended the observation period of those transsexuals who have had unrealistic expectations of the benefits of reassignment surgery. The observation of one medical professional associated with the Clinic that a particular transsexual's

> desire for sex reassignment appears to involve unrealistic expectations ... that it will solve his distress over the inability to relate to others

is the sort of comment frequently encountered in transsexuals' files and in the clinical literature (for example, Townsend 1978: 32; Green 1974: 92). Post-operative transsexuals themselves were aware of the pitfalls of other transsexuals placing too much significance on surgery. One, who is now post-operative and assists in counselling other transsexuals, noted that some saw surgery as a 'cure all' for all the anxieties and problems of the past, such as depression, loneliness and poverty, whereas others saw surgery as an end in itself, with little regard for what could happen afterwards. Another post-operative transsexual who was critical of other's unrealistic expectations of surgery, especially in alleviating problems associated with unemployment, thought that 'it should be compulsory for transsexuals to be in work before surgery is carried out'. A hint of an extreme expectation of surgery was evident in a psychiatrist's remark about a person who was concerned about other transsexuals' totally unrealistic expectations of reassignment surgery. In her file the psychiatrist had noted that

> she felt that they had hoped it [reassignment surgery] would change their lives and when it didn't too many of them died [committed suicide].

A broader picture of factors influencing the recommendation and timing of surgery can be gleaned from the range of good prognostic indicators which were frequently mentioned in the files. These indicators provide something resembling an identikit picture of the Clinic's ideal candidate for reassignment surgery and, conversely, a picture of the poorest. Good prognostic indicators concerning any individual transsexual are:

(a) has no major psychopathology
(b) identifies as a woman and wants to live as such; in childhood this may have manifested itself as embarrassment when undressing in front of other boys
(c) has a long history of cross dressing
(d) has a low sex drive
(e) is young and acknowledges being a transsexual from an early age
(f) is slightly built
(g) was seen as an effeminate boy/youth when younger
(h) was a loner when younger
(i) now has a good social and occupational situation.[19]

Mention of slight build and, possibly, persisting effeminacy, warrant some elaboration because, as observable characteristics, they have an important role in how medical professionals evaluate an individual as a candidate for surgery. Take, for instance, the comments of an endocrinologist with extensive experience in dealing with transsexuals:

there are some, despite their protestations to the contrary, who still appear clumsy and look ill-at-ease or embarrassed, as though they have some difficulty in adopting the role that they claim is rightfully theirs. Their present identity is obviously a new guise. Sometimes it is a bony frame with obvious muscular development that cannot be hidden which leads to doubt about the person's gender. At other times, it may be sheer height, size of hands and feet, and the physical mould in which they are cast that invites exposure of the true biological identity. For some, without cosmetics, there is no confusion of identity, for the facial contour with beard and laryngeal prominence clearly indicate the effect of androgens (male sex hormones), although with cosmetics and judicious dressing the illusion may be nearly perfect. The most distressing patients of all seeking help are those whose bearing, dress, and attitude reveal them to be men awkwardly dressed in women's clothing ... The disparity in clinical presentation emphasizes the fact that some are well-versed and established in their role and others are not (Steinbeck 1986: 68-69).

This passage is quoted at length to demonstrate that being 'well-versed and established' in the role of a woman is not wholly contingent on physical characteristics. Moreover, these same characteristics in different individuals do not necessarily lead to identical perceptions of gender, for clothes, cosmetics and non-'awkward' behaviour, or behaviour associated with women, are also involved in public perceptions of gender. In other words, it may be the case that physical characteristics are not as important as they might appear when taken in isolation. I would suggest, as the passage above illustrates, that the role of physical characteristics is often confounded with other, arguably more important, factors. These factors will be examined at length in the following chapter. In anticipation of that discussion I want briefly to comment on the period of ambiguity which most transsexuals passed through when they started living full time as women.

Given that most transsexuals started female hormones close to their first visit to the Clinic and their decision to live full time as women, they were therefore most ambiguous as women at that time. They themselves were aware of needing to learn skills related to being women, such as dress sense, application of make up and mannerisms. In terms of physical characteristics, however, it was not until months after starting female hormones that visible changes, such as facial hair reduction, breast enlargement, changes in body contour and an alteration in the voice, could be discerned. The period of ambiguity during which transsexuals were not always perceived as women varied because of variation in the effects of hormones and their needing to learn the more subtle aspects of being a woman. The main point of interest here is that ambiguity did not wane entirely because of the effects of female hormones. Repeatedly I saw in transsexuals' files comments from professionals indicating that ambiguity persisted despite dramatic feminising effects of hormones. In other cases there might be no ambiguity even though the effects of hormones were yet to be seen. Clearly, being regarded *as* a woman is not the same as *looking like* a woman. This observation is elaborated in the following chapter which focuses on the micro aspects of the process of becoming a woman.

Finally, it is important to look at the patterned experiences of transsexuals themselves at various points in the acceptance stage, particularly as they approached surgery. All who were about to have surgery clearly conveyed their certainty of the appropriateness of that course of action. Of course, one could argue that this would be the case by definition, for why would the Clinic recommend surgery if a candidate did not want it? This is true, but what needs to be acknowledged is that, in contrast to the younger transsexuals who were notable for agitating for a reduction in the two year waiting period before surgery was contemplated, several transsexuals at an earlier phase in the acceptance stage were not so certain of whether they really wanted to go so far as having such irreversible surgery. What then occurred in the intervening

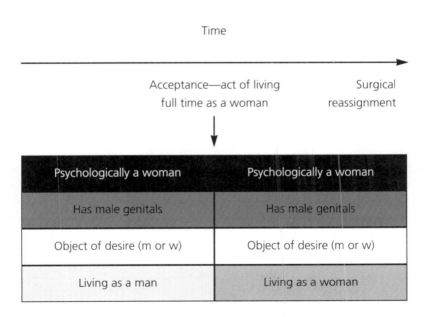

Figure 4:2   *Some patterns of continuity and change associated with living full time as a woman*

period? I suggest that the experience of living as a woman is the critical factor. As figure 4:2 indicates, the obvious change in the major patterns impinging on their lives either side of living as a woman is that experience itself, which is accumulative. By contrast, there is continuity of having male genitals, the object of sexual attraction, and feeling psychologically a woman. This point is consistent with the demise of ambiguity, for just as professionals have commented on the presence of ambiguity in transsexuals' files, they also have noted its demise as particular individuals learn to be women. It is therefore not surprising that, after living a minimum of two years as women, transsexuals generally have no second thoughts about the finality of surgery.

Invisibility

Invisibility is the stage after surgical reassignment when a transsexual makes a conscious attempt to limit the likelihood of public access to information about her recent history. It involves one or more of: moving to another city, changing jobs, severing ties with acquaintances from the past and, particularly, reducing social contacts with other transsexuals. It is accompanied by increasing confidence in being a woman and a degree of taken for granted-ness of one's own gender (cf. Tully 1992: xiv).

This stage is the most difficult to illustrate with good evidence because becoming socially invisible is a matter of degree and the post-operative transsexuals, who constituted about one-third of interviewees in this study, are still in the broad process of becoming women. At the time of writing, they fell into three, not necessarily equal categories. The first were the most socially visible transsexuals who made a point of declaring their transsexuality in public settings, for example, to colleagues in a new work setting, to other students in a university class, to fellow members of a drama group and, in a few instances, to the media. These transsexuals have not entered the stage of invisibility, ostensibly because they have chosen not to or, perhaps in some cases, because they acknowledge the difficulty of successfully 'doing gender' in everyday life.

By contrast, in the earliest stage of invisibility were those less socially visible transsexuals who made the transition to living as women at their, then, current place of work. They were concerned to maintain confidentiality about their background and did not wish to make it any more public than it was. They could not be totally invisible, however, while they maintained their networks at their place of employment.

The least socially visible were those transsexuals who had changed jobs and/or their place of residence and had no everyday contact with people who knew their backgrounds, that is, with the exception of parents and other close family or friends. It was not that these transsexuals did not or could not tell anyone about their transsexuality. Rather, it was that they did not need to. Associated with being among the least visible was a high commitment to work, 'having moved on', as one transsexual put it, and having the highest concern for confidentiality of their background.

This discussion of the macro process of becoming a woman has taken a step back so as to fit the various stages of that process into a range of social contexts, such as the family, work and the Gender Dysphoria Clinic. There have been moments when it would have been worthwhile to get in a little closer to examine the experiences of individuals. Some of those situations were mentioned as foreshadowing the following chapter. The discussion in the section above of the interplay of physical and behavioural factors in attaining and maintaining gender, for example, prompts a change of scope. The following chapter on the micro process of becoming a woman picks up more on those sorts of aspects of the world of transsexuals by focusing on individuals' experiences and social interactions.

NOTES

1 For a more detailed description of the sources of evidence, see chapter one.

2 The issue of relying on transsexuals' memories to retrieve evidence from the past is a part of a larger methodological problem for social scientists. The issue of a vantage point in the present that can distort the nature of the past has been commented on by others in relation to transsexuals; see, for instance, Fisk in Billings and Urban (1982) and Green (1974).

3 'Dominant' is not used loosely here but refers to thematic qualities found in a majority of cases. Themes evident in all cases are 'universal' whereas those found in a minority of cases (but more than 15 per cent) are 'minor' themes.

4 This percentage is a little higher than that found by Tully (1992: 124) among male to female transsexuals (i.e. 46 per cent).

5 Stuart (1983: 24, 53, 126) also talks of marriage as a mechanism to correct the strong desire to be and live as a woman.

6 Other research on male to female transsexuals stresses this same concern about femininity. See, for instance, Ekins (1993: 14ff.) and Hausman (1992: 298).

7 That 'popular language' includes the views transsexuals and transvestites have of each other. As Tully (1992: 255) notes, transsexuals often view transvestites as 'just playing at it', whereas transvestites view transsexuals as 'transvestites with "big ideas"'.

8 See Middleton (1993) and Mostyn (1993).

9 See chapter 2.

10 'Census characteristics of Australia', Australian Bureau of Statistics, catalogue no. 2710.0, p. 17.

11 Cf. Collyer (1994).

12 Of course, in referring to this heterosexual pattern I am treating transsexuals as women.

13 It is worth noting that Stuart (1983: 55) found 52 per cent of male to female transsexuals to be heterosexual in their role as women, the remainder being bisexual and lesbian. By comparison, Bentler (quoted in Ross 1986a: 4) claims that male to female transsexuals in his study were heterosexual, homosexual and asexual in equal proportions. Tully (1992: 243), on the other hand, believed 'asexual' transsexuals to be 'not common'.

14 Other 'asexual' responses included statements such as 'I have no steady partner, nor has there been one and nor is there likely to be one' and 'I don't care if my vagina is short. It's not going to be doing anything' (a comment made after surgery). Cf. Tully (1992: 124).

15 See especially King (1993: 185ff.); Stuart (1983); Harding (1986: 115); and Grimm (1987: 68).

16 Thirty-three was the median age for interviewees and only one was that age in 1993.

17 This figure includes the 14 per cent of students.

18 Although younger transsexuals voiced their desire for a shorter than two year waiting period, in practice it has only happened in a couple of instances I am aware of. One was a transsexual who had come from another city where she had lived as a woman for at least a year and was under the care of a sympathetic psychiatrist.

19 Concerning other attempts to list good and poor prognostic indicators for surgery, see for example Brown (1990: 61).

5
The Micro Process of Becoming a Woman

'I was still the same. Knowing myself yet being someone other'
T. S. Eliot

The micro process of becoming a woman concentrates more on individuals' understandings of their own situations. This is not to say that there are no patterns at this level. There are, but the focus is more on those at the individual level rather than those broad patterns in the six stages of the macro process of becoming a woman.

By focusing on individuals, it is possible to clarify some of the questions raised in chapter two, such as: why is belonging to one sex and having the psychological identity of the other such an unstable state? And, to what extent is it an assumption that biological or 'natural' difference is more 'real' for transsexuals than social or learned attributes? Answers, in turn, will assist in addressing wider questions, such as, are 'male' and 'female', 'men' and 'women' absolute categories or are they socially and histori-cally constructed? And to what extent is transsexualism a social construction? The latter is related to the question of whether transsexualism challenges existing categories of gender or rein-forces them and raises the provocative question: are transsexuals a third gender?[1]

Transsexuals' Approach to Gender

Applying the notions of sex and gender to transsexuals is a worthwhile exercise, for these people help to clarify what those concepts mean in everyday life. Garber (1993: 110) is certainly perceptive in saying that transsexuals are more interested in the notions of maleness, femaleness, masculine and feminine than people who are not transsexual. They are not interested in 'unisex' or 'androgyny' as erotic styles but in gender marked and gender coded identity structures. What then can their experiences tell us? Let us begin by looking at transsexuals' own understanding of gender and what it means to be a woman in a variety of social contexts.

When I began this research I assumed that transsexuals 'passed' to a greater or lesser extent as women and that passing largely depended on the extent to which one had certain conventional attributes of feminine beauty. In other words, I assumed the well-known transsexual Caroline Cossey passed easily as a woman, whereas others who were not as fortunate were less successful and that was that! I might add that I thought about the notion of passing in a somewhat cursory fashion and that it has taken much scrutiny of my ideas and research notes to be able to say what my original assumptions were. Of course, I now realise that I brought more than one erroneous assumption to this research. The first, as noted in the previous chapter, was that passing is not the appropriate concept to capture the image of transsexuals' own approach to their gender. Passing implies deception and, given transsexuals' own understanding of themselves, their public presentation of themselves as women is not deception.[2] Second, I now realise my assumption that being seen as a woman is contingent on correspondence to conventional attributes of femininity was mistaken and largely a part of my own taken for granted approach to gender. I and the rest of our society do not routinely reflect on or scrutinise gender and, hence, in everyday life the means by which we know someone to be a man or a woman is not something we consciously weigh up. We may be mistaken, as I clearly was, when we consciously reflect on what constitutes gender. Like most aspects of life we take for granted, it is not until the 'normality' of events is disrupted or violated do we see that we have been taking gender for granted or adopting a 'natural attitude.' The natural attitude to gender suggests that the notion of 'doing gender', which was outlined in chapter two, is clearly the most productive way of understanding how transsexuals, as biological males, approach the task of living as women.

The natural attitude is not peculiar to gender but applies to any social situation that needs to be sustained and managed but which, at the same time, is taken for granted by participants. Joan Emerson's (1970) account of the gynecological examination, for example, illustrates how an everyday, taken for granted medical procedure is actually a precarious exercise and therefore requires managing. Provided it is managed successfully, then participants take it for granted as 'normal'. Saying that such a situation proceeds normally is to say that its taken for grantedness is a human construction and not a property intrinsic to the event. In terms of what is required to maintain the normality of the gynecological examination, doctors and patients often have different priorities, albeit implicit. Whereas it is important for doctors to keep patients 'in line' by not letting them show any sexual arousal, some patients see having a clean body and underwear as more significant. What all this is saying is that, in approaching gender, what is perceived as the priority in maintaining the normality or taken for grantedness of the moment can vary among people.[3]

Applying the notion of 'doing gender' to transsexuals who have made the transition to living as women, a few questions emerge which are worth pursuing. Given the emphasis on process in the previous chapter, to what extent do transsexuals learn how gender is 'done' in everyday life? Do some learn better than others? Also, what do we learn about gender from the practice of transsexuals 'doing' it?

My own experience of interviewing and re-interviewing transsexuals provides some of the answers. My first insight was discovering that some transsexuals who, based on their file photographs, looked like other women of the same age, were not necessarily convincing as women when we actually met. Why was this so? This experience has links to the discussion of ambiguity in the previous chapter, where I made the claim that being *regarded* as a woman was not the same as *looking* like a woman. That comment, however, was based on written notes in transsexuals' files. What is it about actual interaction that leads us to regard anyone, particularly a male to female transsexual, as a woman?

The presentation of self as a woman

A photograph conveys a broad idea of a transsexual's body and clothing, admittedly two important factors I will discuss shortly, but it bypasses what I now believe to be the key factor in creating and sustaining the public's taken for granted assumption of a transsexual's and, for that matter, any individual's gender. That factor is the individual's own confident presentation of self as a *woman* in everyday situations, such as shopping, chatting to acquaintances, and dealing with staff in government departments. In those situations, 'small behaviours' or characteristic mannerisms and gestures serve as gender cues provided they are carried out confidently. An aspect of confident behaviour is the individual transsexual's skill in recognising, possibly unconsciously, that the public's perception of gender coded behaviour is at the taken for granted level.

Transsexuals' own accounts of their social experiences corroborate my assessment that the confident presentation of self is the key factor in shaping the public's recognition of a transsexual's gender. Specifically, this is evident in the variety of everyday situations in which transsexuals said they felt comfortable and uncomfortable about their gender. Figure 5:1 indicates the sorts of situations in each of four categories, that is, comfortable and uncomfortable situations in which other persons were known and not known. This figure provides some useful insights but its principal limitation is that it does not convey the overwhelming concentration of transsexuals' comfortable and uncomfortable feelings in situations where other people were *not* known. With this caveat in mind, it nevertheless clarifies the importance of the public's natural attitude to gender and the significance of its disruption.

In those situations in the top right cell, the nature of interaction in each case confirms the other person's taken for granted assumption of the transsexual's gender. There was a dominant pattern among interviewees of their giving spontaneous accounts of feeling 'good' in public situations, such as shopping and being

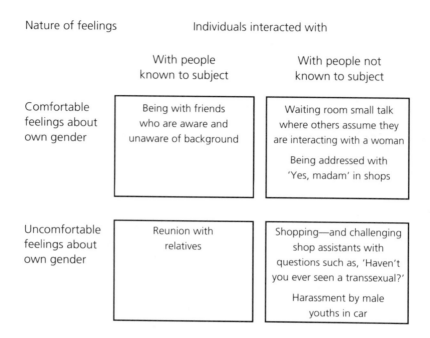

Nature of feelings	Individuals interacted with	
	With people known to subject	With people not known to subject
Comfortable feelings about own gender	Being with friends who are aware and unaware of background	Waiting room small talk where others assume they are interacting with a woman Being addressed with 'Yes, madam' in shops
Uncomfortable feelings about own gender	Reunion with relatives	Shopping—and challenging shop assistants with questions such as, 'Haven't you ever seen a transsexual?' Harassment by male youths in car

Figure 5:1   *Transsexuals' feelings in specific social interactions*

addressed as 'madam' by shop assistants or sitting in waiting rooms and engaging in small talk with other women. A pre-operative transsexual in her mid-forties, whom I shall call Jackie, described a variant of the latter situation. She related, in what might have appeared a trivial moment to anyone else, an incident that made her feel 'really good' about her capacity to be a convincing woman. She was alone in the waiting room at the Clinic before a routine consultation. Two young girls came into the room and sat down in the nearest seats that happened to be alongside Jackie. The girls continued with their conversation, which happened to touch on menstruation. Jackie recalled that that made her feel very comfortable because the girls took it for granted that she was a woman: 'If they had seen me as a guy in a dress then they wouldn't have sat next to me and talked about their periods'. This instance is typical of the comfortable, everyday situations concerning gender mentioned by other transsexuals. Generally, they saw them as comfortable because, although apparently trivial, they *knew* at the time they were being taken for granted as women.

The picture to this point demonstrates three important aspects associated with 'doing gender'. The first is that it primarily involves interaction. The second aspect is that success involves doing gender at the taken for granted level of interaction where participants are generally not acutely aware of what they are doing. Third, success at doing gender does not necessarily depend on personal appearances. All this raises an important issue, for all transsexuals think about gender more than the wider community and, being aware of their history of gender confusion, approach being women with varying degrees of awareness of their own gendered behaviour. Is this awareness associated with degrees of competence at doing gender? This question is a difficult one but some indication of the answer can be gleaned from an examination of situations in which transsexuals experienced uncomfortable feelings about gender.

Uncomfortable feelings sprang from situations in which transsexuals were aware their gender was not being taken for granted. Anna, a pre-operative transsexual who, on the basis of a photograph, seemed very convincing as a woman, related a history of feeling uncomfortable and self-conscious about her gender when shopping. It appears her self-consciousness had frequently been noticed by shop assistants, who, in turn, conveyed their own awkwardness in negotiating transactions. Anna described how her shopping experiences often ended in disappointment. She would be browsing in a store and would happen to catch the shop assistant's eye. Immediately she would look away thinking 'I wonder whether she's sprung me'. The resulting embarrassment would invite an awkward question from the shop assistant, such as 'Are you feeling all right?' or 'Is there anything I can do to help?' This would reinforce Anna's self-consciousness and trigger the defensive, angry question: 'Haven't you ever seen a transsexual?' Clearly Anna did not 'do' gender well, largely because she was unnecessarily self-conscious about her public presentation of self that attracted the attention of the public. In her case, violation of the taken for grantedness of gender made the public conscious of what they otherwise would not have noticed.

A further indication of this violation is the way medical professionals have perceived transsexuals in terms of their ability to do gender. The range of comments about routine consultations recorded in the Clinic's files indicated a range of violations by transsexuals of the taken for grantedness of their gender. The most frequent observation, at one end of the range, was the comment that a particular transsexual presented as a 'convincing' or 'reasonably convincing' woman. This type of assessment did not necessarily stem from a transsexual's feminine appearance. In several cases a 'convincing' woman was middle aged, overweight and/or 'not very feminine in appearance'. Those transsexuals who were 'unconvincing' violated to some extent professionals' own taken for granted approaches to gender. Their manner rather than their appearance was the trigger. One transsexual, for instance, prompted the comment that

> she has not mastered the art of being a very feminine woman in spite of a very pleasing appearance.

Referring to another, a psychologist noted that

> from appearance [X] came across as a woman. However, [X's] general manner was not very feminine.[4]

At the other end of the range, another psychologist conveyed the awkwardness of a consultation with a transsexual whose disruption of the taken for grantedness of gender led to the comment that

> it was difficult to relate to *him* as a female as *his* mannerisms and behaviour were more typically masculine than feminine [emphasis added].

Similarly, another professional recorded that

> [Y] came in today dressed as a woman but clearly came across as a man in a dress and I felt very uncomfortable.

One of my interviewees asked me, after we had discussed this violation of the taken for grantedness of gender, whether doing gender was a little like being a successful shop lifter. It is an unfortunate metaphor but it is a good one and, therefore, worth elaborating. Inexperienced shop lifters who are self-conscious about what they are about to do seem to send out cues to others, especially security staff watching them on closed circuit television. Violation of the taken for grantedness of the relaxed shopper alerts onlookers to what they otherwise would not notice. The successful shop lifter is the person who can adopt the 'natural' poise of shopping while shoplifting. When leaving the store this confidence may even extend to asking security guards whether they have problems with shop lifters! If such people get away with their crime it is because no one would ever question that they are anything other than what they appear to be. Like all metaphors, though, this one has its limitations in illustrating transsexuals doing gender. Unlike the transsexual, the shop lifter is 'passing' as an ordinary shopper, that is, engaging in deception.

It is worth noting that a few transsexuals described uncomfortable feelings about their gender when harassed by young men cruising the streets in cars. This is worth noting because in each of those cases the unpleasant feelings did not arise because they had been 'sprung' or identified as male to female transsexuals. Notwithstanding the gratuitous nature of the situation for any woman, the uncomfortable feelings arose from the perception that those men *might* have sensed that they were harassing a transsexual and, moreover, that being a transsexual invited the harassment. It is difficult to verify what actually occurred in those situations but, arguably, self-consciousness about gender can lead to visible cues in dress and behaviour that invite unwelcome attention.

By contrast, transsexuals' interactions with people they knew did not lead to the same concentration of accounts of comfortable and uncomfortable feelings about gender. Nevertheless, in those situations the natural attitude to gender persisted. When close friends were not aware that one of their number was a transsexual, their implicit acceptance of her as a woman was, at the same time, a confirmation of the natural attitude and a comfortable situation. In situations where friends were aware of a transsexual's background, the comfortable feelings sprang from acceptance and support rather than from specific feelings about gender. Similarly, having uncomfortable feelings among people who were known personally, such as meeting relatives for the first time as a woman, stemmed from the awkwardness of the moment rather than from difficulties in maintaining the natural attitude to gender.

Clothes, the body and the company one keeps

I mentioned earlier that clothes and the body are also important in influencing the public's natural attitude to gender. From transsexuals' accounts of their social interactions, those factors were obviously secondary to the confident presentation of self as women, although not all consciously recognised this point. Again, some of those transsexuals who, on the basis of their photograph, I would have imagined having difficulty in negotiating everyday situations as women because of their masculine bodies, were convincing in their presentation of self at interview and related none of the difficulties in everyday life touched on earlier. This is not to say that transsexuals living as women who have what they might think are explicit male body characteristics, such as above average body size, facial hair, and muscular development, do not attract scrutiny. They do, for *any* woman over two metres tall, for example, will attract 'double takes' from the public. If, however, those transsexuals' presentation of themselves as women is confident and convincing, then the public do not resort to explanations, such as 'that person must be a transsexual'. Should a conscious explanation emerge, it is more likely to be something like 'some women are tall' or 'some women have facial hair'.

Clothes can also be the source of public scrutiny because of violation of what is anticipated in particular settings. As one transsexual put it,

> if you wear a cocktail dress down to the corner store at 10am to get a carton of milk, then you're inviting prying looks.

Cocktail dresses seem to be something of a yardstick in assessing the nature of the occasion, for Matto (1974: 207) makes the same point about recognition of transsexuals' over-dressing:

one physician stated that a newly operated upon woman might come into his office for counseling in a cocktail dress more appropriate for the theatre.

In these sorts of situations though, provided there is a confident presentation of self as a woman, the public explanation would more than likely be 'maybe she's on her way to a formal lunch' rather than 'that's a transsexual in a cocktail dress!'

Finally, the other factor influencing the public's natural attitude to gender, and thus any transsexual being a convincing woman, is the company a transsexual keeps. Irrespective of the successful presentation of self as a woman, the nature of the body and the clothes one puts on it, being seen in the company of transsexuals who do attract public scrutiny, or people who frequently use the wrong pronouns, were minor themes in accounts of being 'read' or 'sprung', that is, identified as a transsexual.

Mention of these factors influencing the public's perception of transsexuals as women brings us back to the question surrounding variation in the confident presentation of self. Do transsexuals learn to be convincing women?

In the discussion of ambiguity in the previous chapter I made the point that ambiguity of transsexuals' gender persisted in some cases despite the feminising effects of female hormones. In other cases, there was no ambiguity of gender even though the effects of hormones were not apparent. In short, being *regarded* as a woman was not the same as *looking like* a woman. On the basis of comments by Clinic staff in transsexuals' files, individuals initially seen as ambiguous or unconvincing were almost always later regarded as more convincing women. In one case, for example, a transsexual was initially judged to be 'passing poorly' and 'unconvincing' as a woman and one year later was seen to be 'much more convincing as a woman'. My own experience of interviewing transsexuals many times, and in some cases over a period of one and a half years, corresponds with these comments. I saw five people make the transition within the acceptance stage to living full time as women and, in each case, their success at doing gender improved over time. All this is limited evidence of some form of learning to do gender but it is difficult to say precisely what form that learning takes. There are, however, two aspects of this process that are worth noting. First, competence in doing gender sprang primarily from doing it. Transsexuals recognised themselves that, in the taken for granted nature of gender attribution in everyday life, self-consciousness led to violation of that taken for grantedness. Put differently, they learned from their successful and comfortable encounters involving gender that being confident and relaxed works. Second, in some cases transsexuals simply reached the point of not worrying any longer what people thought about their presentation of self, which of course then enabled them to be more relaxed in doing gender.

As figure 4:2 in the previous chapter demonstrated, alongside the continuities either side of the decision to live as a woman, the actual experience of doing it was the significant change and the key aspect of gaining certainty about the prospect of surgery as well as learning to do gender. This is indirectly corroborated by a minor pattern of reservation evident among transsexuals who, at the time of interview, had not made the transition to living full time as women. Of all transsexuals interviewed they:

(a) were the most unsure about the prospect of reassignment surgery;

(b) were the least confident about how they looked when presenting as women;

(c) were the most unsure about whether they had the skills to live successfully as women; and

(d) were the most concerned about what others thought.

One of those transsexuals conveyed her awareness of the gap she had to bridge. She related how her frequent communication with a fellow computer enthusiast—a man—through electronic mail gave her the feelings she hoped she would someday experience 'out there on the street' interacting with people, but as a woman. She added that, not having met the person she communicated with, 'I was able to be myself and be treated as a woman at the same time'.

In summary, transsexuals' confident presentation of themselves as women as the principal factor in the public's attribution of their gender provides further confirmation of the advantages of viewing gender more as a process or managed accomplishment than a quality. As I have already indicated, this point is not new and has been stressed by social scientists such as Garfinkel (Garfinkel and Stoller 1967), Kessler and McKenna (1985),[5] Devor (1989: 146-147) and more recently by Giddens (1991). The latter captures the relationship between the body and gender and is worth quoting in concluding this point:

> how should we think of the body in relation to its sexual char-
> acteristics? Nothing is clearer than that gender is a matter of
> learning and continuous 'work', rather than a simple extension
> of biologically given sexual difference. In respect of this aspect
> of the body, we can return to the central themes of eth-
> nomethodology as elaborated by Garfinkel. Ethnomethodology
> has become so closely identified with conversation analysis that
> it is easily forgotten that Garfinkel's work developed out of
> a direct concern with the managing of gender. The case
> of Agnes, the transsexual ... shows that to be a 'man' or a
> 'woman' depends on a chronic monitoring of the body and
> bodily gestures. There is in fact no single bodily trait which
> separates all women from all men. Only those few individuals
> who have something like a full experience of being a member
> of both sexes can completely appreciate how pervasive are the
> details of bodily display and management by which gender is
> 'done'(1991: 63).

This approach to gender, however, poses something of a problem. If, in light of transsexuals' concern with reassignment surgery and their strong desire to approximate the biological sex characteristics of females, having a female body is not *the* critical factor in doing gender then why is it important? Although in everyday social interaction we generally do not use those sex differences to attribute gender and although we do not interact with unclothed, whole bodies, it would be a mistake to assume that the body assumes minor importance in transsexuals' consciousness. The body warrants closer examination because its role centres on more than how it is immediately perceived by others, whether, for example, a transsexual is tall or short or fat or thin. There is also the significance of what the body means to transsexuals themselves and the important place reassignment surgery assumes in transsexuals' lives. The following section turns to the significance of the body and touches on areas not dealt with in other research.

The Body and the Transsexual

'The body' is not an exact concept in sociology, as Bertholet (1991) notes in a well-known book on the subject. In asking what does the term refer to, Berthelot observes that 'the body seems to be taken for granted and ... appears to constitute a self-evident fact' (1991: 391). Arguably, an aspect of this self-evident nature of the body is the holistic way it is regarded in the socio-logical literature (see Gatens 1983). Transsexuals' orientations to the body, however, revealed a more complex picture that centred on the importance of the body in two coexisting discourses—the social and individual. These discourses are compared in figure 5:2 and need some elaboration.

Social discourse on the body
Transsexuals' social discourse stressed the importance of genitalia, especially as the means of attributing gender at birth and in social contexts such as advertising. This stress is consistent with the wider social view that biological endowments at birth are impor-tant and immutable and are just logical precursors, in the case of females, to breast development, the absence of facial hair, a high pitched voice, and feminine gendered behaviour. Summarised by Connell's comment that 'society registers what nature decrees' (1987: 67) this view was also the dominant assumption in the academic literature that claims, for example, 'that fundamentally gender is a consequence of a biological blueprint' (Kessler and McKenna 1985: viii). For this reason the social discourse could also be referred to as the 'biology is destiny' discourse. However, this social discourse has more implicit dimensions that are evident in a comparison of the 'superficial' and 'deep' structures in trans-sexuals' approach to sex and gender. Concerning superficial structure, we have already noted that transsexuals are more inter-ested in the notions of maleness, femaleness, masculine and feminine than people who are not transsexual. As Garber put it,

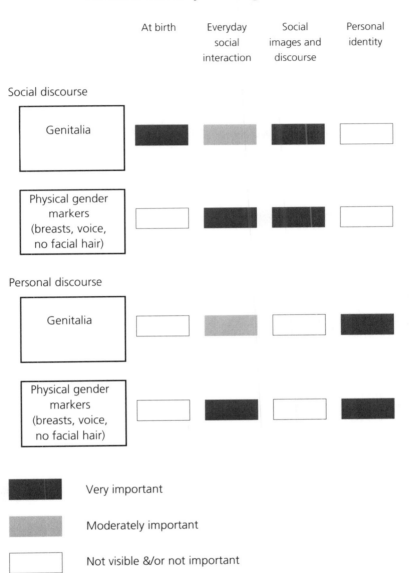

Figure 5:2   *Importance of the body in social and personal discourses*

they have a stake in gender marked and gender coded identity structures (1993: 110). This was borne out among the transsexuals in this study. Their history of gender confusion was generally associated with a reflective and critical approach to the question 'What is gender?' Many had 'read up' on recent literature on sex and gender in relation to transsexualism and, in one way or another, had given those concepts considerable thought. All were painfully aware that sex and gender are not synonymous and, by definition, no one believed that sex determines gender. In contrast to the wider public's natural attitude to gender and its relation to the body, the sex–gender relationship was not something transsexuals took for granted. Wells, herself a transsexual, illustrates this point.

> In William Golding's novel *Free Fall*, a young man asks the woman he is in love with, 'What is it like to be you?' At least one psychiatrist has quoted the passage to illustrate the normal curiosity we all have about what it must be like to be someone else. Far more significant for me was the girl's reply: 'Just ordinary'. I remember when I read it, thinking how wonderful it would be to feel like that—whole, integrated, all-of-a-piece, ordinary. And to be able to take it for granted! It was almost too much for me to comprehend, since all my life I had felt myself to be very un-ordinary. Unlike the girl in Golding's novel (and, it seemed to me, the rest of the world), I was at total odds with my body, a person divided. To all appearances I was male. But I knew I was female (1986: 9).

At this level I call 'superficial structure', transsexuals differ from the wider society because of this clearly observable, reflective approach to notions of sex and gender. This is simply another way of saying that their everyday thinking about sex and gender is patterned, as is the absence of that sort of reflection among the public, who largely take it for granted that sex determines gender. Among transsexuals and the public, those patterns are superficial structures because of their ease of location (see figure 5:3).

	Critical approach	Natural attitude
Superficial structure of approach to sex and gender	**Transsexuals** Gender is distinct from sex. No relationship drawn with biological sex	**Public** Relationship between sex and gender is taken for granted. The former determines the latter
Deep structure of approach to sex and gender	**Selected scholars** Gender, sex and sexual orientation are involved in many relationships, e.g. Grimm	**Transsexuals & public** Gender and sex should correspond

Figure 5:3 *Transsexuals' and public's approach to sex and gender*

There is, however, another, less obvious structure. As transsexuals' social discourse reveals, they are also a part of the wider society and share with the wider public certain implicit responses towards sex and gender. Although they do not collapse the notions of sex and gender or believe they are causally related, all transsexuals implicitly assumed that they *should* at least correspond. By 'correspond' they meant if one were psychologically a woman then the body should conform to that state. As figure 5:3 conveys, transsexuals and the wider public share this similar deep structured, taken for granted assumption of (or a natural attitude towards) the need for a correspondence of sex and gender. It is a deep structure because few transsexuals and members of the public consciously reflect on their assumption or its significance. This is borne out, for example, in the difficulty people have in understanding why they do not and cannot regard a 'sex change' as being in a similar category to, say, cosmetic surgery on the nose or breasts. As Garber notes, the former

> represents the dislocation of everything we conventionally 'know' or believe about gender identities and gender roles, 'male' and 'female' subjectivities (1993: 117).

Predictably, in the course of this study, transsexuals did not spontaneously offer this deep structured assumption concerning sex and gender as something they believed in and, hence, it was not easily observed. When I introduced it into discussions, however, no one denied the obvious necessity of sex and gender corresponding, a point implicitly supported by the frequent comment that reassignment surgery is important so that one can feel 'complete'. No one proposed or even hinted at a relationship between sex and gender that allowed for an array of psychosexual identities as outlined by Grimm (1987) and discussed in chapter two. Arguably, this deep structure of the relationship of sex and gender among the public helps explain the stigma attached to reassignment surgery in medical circles (see King 1993: 88-89; Collyer 1994; Billings and Urban 1982).

Personal discourse on the body

By contrast, the personal discourse among transsexuals acknowledged that although the genitals were significant, other aspects of the body, such as breasts, voice and facial hair, were more important in everyday interaction, especially if gender reassignment surgery was not imminent. In this discourse, the genitals assumed more symbolic, negative significance in individuals' accounts alongside attempts to block out their existence, even in private. Not handling the genitals, avoiding male-style masturbation and sitting to urinate, even when at home, were frequently mentioned. In social interaction the genitals were important only to the extent that individual transsexuals were involved, or may have been involved, in a close relationship, be it with a homosexual or heterosexual partner. Where they were in intimate relationships, pre-operative transsexuals often described covering their genitals when engaging in sexual activity and having a pact with their lovers to avoid touching those parts.[6] The desire to be rid of the genitals—that is, to 'be complete' as a woman—was also moderately important in avoiding those few awkward social interactions that were largely out of one's control, such as unwelcomed interruptions from shop assistants when trying on clothes, trying to change in the public dressing room at a swimming pool, or having to be undressed in a hospital following an accident.

It is important, however, to stress the contextual nature of the social and personal discourses. Figuratively speaking, the social discourse, with the significance it places on the genitals, formed an ever present background for transsexuals. Despite the superficial structure of their critical approach to the nature of and relationship between sex and gender, the deep structure of the necessity of their correspondence was a key part of their personal identity and at the same time a dominant theme in their stressing the importance of bringing the body into line with the mind through reassignment surgery.

On the other hand, to the pre-operative transsexual waiting or being assessed for surgery, the social discourse was less prominent because of the greater foreground importance in everyday life of doing something about developing and maintaining the primary gender markers, in particular, removing facial hair, cultivating an acceptable female voice and, in some cases, seeking surgical intervention for breast augmentation. These assumed greater everyday importance because they are among the key physical markers by which gender is communicated in public.[7] In other words, transsexuals were aware that success in doing gender meant not violating the public's taken for granted assumptions of gender by having masculinised facial hair, a deep voice and, possibly, no breast development. The sort of comment that was a dominant theme among pre-operative transsexuals and one that supports the greater importance of the more pragmatic, personal discourse in their particular context, was offered by one transsexual nearing completion of two years living full time as a woman:

> Look, of course having surgery is important. I feel it is important to be complete ... but it's not everything. There's nothing I can do to hurry it up. In the meantime I have to get on with

life, especially completing electrolysis so that I can get a different job and work as a woman. If it came to the crunch and surgery for this suddenly stopped, I would rather go on living as I am than go back to being a man. Really, at the moment I'm doing alright.

What then are these discourses telling us? Apart from the general comment that in both discourses the concept of the body is not a holistic entity but more a selection of body zones that have varying importance depending on the context, there is an important point that clarifies further our understanding of sex and gender. Although these two discourses are not independent of each other, the personal discourse springs more from transsexuals' everyday experience whereas the social discourse is more an indication of wider understanding of the social significance of the body. To the extent that transsexuals are of the social world they help constitute, it would be a mistake to assume that they do not subscribe to and believe both discourses. The difficulty is knowing which discourse is being used at any one time. It could be the case, for example, that if these two discourses were not acknowledged, that during routine follow ups health professionals might hear transsexuals' accounts of an extreme loathing of the genitals and attribute far more significance to that orientation than it warrants. Researchers such as Stoller (1968), and others who have continued with his assumptions (for example, Millot 1990: 12, 49), might have taken a less phallocentric view of transsexuals' approach to the body if they had acknowledged both the social and personal discourses. By contrast, other commentators such as Money (1988: 89) and Harding (1986: 116) acknowledge in different ways the range and importance of other body parts which are important to transsexuals. It is noteworthy that Harding, as a social worker with many years experience working with transsexuals, should note that the voice and beard are the 'most troublesome' features for male to female transsexuals. Money also emphasises the importance of the voice and beard but includes transsexuals' concern about becoming a 'eunuch' (that is, having no testes, penis or scrotum) and growing the hair long.

I suggest that Harding and Money stressed the features they did because of their vantage points and, therefore, recognition of different or additional evidence from that observed by Stoller. Without engaging in amateur psychiatry, the significance Stoller saw transsexuals attaching to genitalia might have been more a sign of their involvement in a doctor–patient setting echoing a wider social discourse focused on the significance of genitalia. Arguably, from that vantage point Stoller may not have been able to see other evidence suggestive of transsexuals' pragmatic concern for other parts of the body in the everyday practice of being a woman, that is, their personal discourse.

When the relative use of these two discourses is looked at closely, there is a clear pattern. Use of social discourse to account for feelings and priorities was more evident among pre-operative transsexuals with lower levels of education and from manual occupations. They expressed the strongest loathing of their genitals and experienced the most urgent desire to have reassignment surgery.[8] They were also the individuals who saw the priority of obvious breast development and, hence, the attraction of breast augmentation surgery, and in almost every case wanted a sexual relationship with a heterosexual man.

By contrast, more educated transsexuals in a range of professional occupations stressed the pragmatic nature of their lives and used the personal discourse to account for their feelings and priorities. They spoke, for instance, in more qualified terms about the importance of reassignment surgery and the need to put that prospect into the background so that they could get on with their lives as women, which may or may not have had a place for a lover who was not necessarily a man. This sort of discourse was typified by the comment from a pre-operative transsexual, that

the genitals can wait, it's the body which is important ... to have good legs and bottom, long hair and no facial hair.

In summary then, the varying extent to which these two co-existing discourses are invoked by transsexuals may be a direct result of the amount of education a person has had. The assumption is that the more education people receive, the more they scrutinise and question wider, social assumptions and become less prone to accepting so-called popular truths. On the other hand, the association of these discourses with education levels may be more a measure of the extent to which more educated people were relaxed and honest when being interviewed by someone with a similar background.

To this point transsexuals doing gender implicates the body through the social and personal discourses and the superficial and deep structures involving the relationship between sex and gender. There is also the additional dimension of the sort of body transsexuals want, namely a body that corresponds to some notion of an ideal image of femininity or, as Harding (1986: 115) puts it, an 'exaggerated view of womanliness'. These dimensions, although analytically distinct, are bound together in reality. In the minds of transsexuals they are difficult to separate, as the spontaneous comment from one pre-operative transsexual indicated in response to my question about what she wanted from the Clinic:

> it's a *woman's* body I want, the *female* look ... to be treated as a *woman* and feel wholly *feminine* [emphasis added].

This aspiration to the conventional image of the feminine woman was the dominant pattern among transsexuals and helps explain why their perceived discrepancy between sex and gender is so psychologically unsettling.

This discussion has addressed most of the questions posed at the beginning of this chapter. In clarifying how transsexuals and the wider public approach the concepts of sex and gender, it seems obvious that transsexuals reinforce existing gender categories rather than challenge them. They want to preserve existing gender differences and, hence, are more conservative than radical in terms of their psychosexual identities. This undermines the claim that transsexuals are a third gender. So far I have not explicitly addressed either the question of whether biological difference is more real than socially learned attributes or Garber's provocative response that gender is causally prior to biological sex differences. Such a claim cannot stand unchallenged, if only because it treats gender differences as if they had no cause. This issue will be taken up when considering factors influencing maintenance of the heterosexual man–woman dichotomy in the final chapter. Before turning to that discussion, the claim that transsexuals are not a third gender but reinforce the existing gender dichotomy prompts an examination of the view proposed by feminists such as Singer (1977) and Devor (1987; 1989) that gender is a continuous concept rather than an array of categories. Without putting too fine a point on the precise number of categories, this is a claim I want to contest. I shall do this by examining the transsexuals' understandings of gender alongside their patterns of sexual desire.

Gender and Sexual Desire

I deliberately use the concept 'sexual desire' because, as noted earlier, determining whether any individual is involved in a physical sexual relationship and, if so, the nature of that relationship is not that straightforward. The history and patterns of individuals' sexual desire, however, are a little more accessible. By looking at transsexuals' understanding of their gender alongside sexual desire I want to address the question of whether their self-understanding and patterns of desire are saying anything about the inappropriateness of the dominant gender dichotomy of heterosexual men and women.

The short answer is that transsexuals reveal a lot about the unrealistic nature of that dichotomy. A watertight argument positing an alternative would require evidence about the wider population I, unfortunately, do not have. What follows is, therefore, somewhat speculative. As chapter two indicated, cross cultural studies of gender and sexual desire demonstrate that certain practices, such as ritualised homosexuality, are integral to a wide variety of societies and cannot be explained by simply claiming their departure from ethical standards, least of all our own. Green (1974: 13) makes the point that atypical sex role adoption, as illustrated by the berdache, has historically been integrated into a wide variety of societies that have created specialised roles for that behaviour. He notes, though, that 'contemporary Western society has been less tolerant of atypical sex-role adoption' (1974: 13). Notwithstanding the current levels of tolerance in our society, increasing visibility of people who are seen as transsexuals alongside the very visible gay and lesbian presence prompts the conclusion that the limited categories of heterosexual man and woman are incapable of coping with what has been a relatively invisible diversity of gender orientations and sexual desires. In short, that dichotomy does not match reality. This point is not exactly novel, for Tully's research among transsexuals in the United Kingdom prompted the following comment:

> the day to day experiences of those whose sexuality is problematic are diffuse and do not provide a neat fit between public categories and private meanings. Historically, for example, the use of the term 'homosexual' to describe a type of person, only became current in the last century (1992: 241).[9]

Transsexuals' self-understanding and patterns of desire help clarify the unrealistic nature of the gender dichotomy. This is somewhat ironic because at the same time they reinforce the gender categories of that dichotomy rather than challenge them. By 'reinforce' I mean acting consistent with the deep structured assumption that if one is a 'woman' then one should have a female body and not only a female body but ideally a *feminine* female body. I deliberately use 'reinforce' rather than 'conform to' because the latter implies some conscious awareness of one's actions. Transsexuals' and the public's natural attitude to that deep structured assumption suggests otherwise. This point is often not fully appreciated by researchers who focus on the unrealistic nature of the dichotomous image of gender. Acknowledging the wide range of psychosexual identities among people, they often appear to be blaming transsexuals for conforming to the very gender dichotomy they have not been able to live within. This point is an aspect of what I call the analysis of hope and will be discussed more in the final chapter.

What then do transsexuals' self-understanding and patterns of desire tell us? Principally, they indicate two key points. First, transsexuals' psychosexual identities are among a range of other identities, such as heterosexual man and homosexual woman, and their transsexualism is the way of adjusting to the perceived social impossibility of living and being accepted as what Grimm (1987) would describe as a 'woman with a penis'.[10] Most people outwardly assume the identity of their socialisation, because of their assumption that sex determines gender and thus psychosexual identity. Many of those individuals though, as transsexuals demonstrate, quietly experience anxiety because their biology 'requires' that they fit either side of the gender dichotomy, that is heterosexual man or woman. Second, transsexuals' self-understanding and patterns of desire also tell us that they are not a third gender but conform to existing expectations of feminine women. Both of these points become clearer in a closer look at the nature of transsexuals' psychosexual desire.

Transsexuals' accounts of the nature of their sexual relationships indicate that their early self-understanding often sprang from how they interpreted those relationships. As we have seen, transsexuals who are now homosexual or heterosexual women have been constant in their attraction to women or men.[11] What has changed with their acceptance of and transition to being women is their own understanding and acceptance of their psychosexual identity. Transsexuals who now have a lesbian orientation, for instance, previously, when living as men, attempted to see themselves as heterosexual men attracted to heterosexual women. Now they see themselves as lesbians. It is important, though, to stress that, alongside the constancy of the object of their attraction, it is not as if their own identities underwent a sudden change when they decided to live full time as women. Although often surrounded by anxiety, confusion and lack of confidence, those identities often predated the public transition to living as women. This is most evident in their accounts of the development of their sex lives. Those transsexuals who, as married men, had sexual difficulties, wanted to be regarded as women by their wives and often resorted to fantasy to make sexual intercourse possible. Similarly, transsexuals who previously were attracted to men and participated in the 'gay scene', did so with varying degrees of difficulty because they generally believed they were not gay and wanted their male partners to see them as women. This picture corresponds with Tully's assessment of the relationship between gender and sexual desire among transsexuals:

many transsexuals of both sexes had early encounters with other people of the same biological sex. However, a homosexual construction placed on these activities became increasingly intolerable as a cross gender identity developed, because such an act 'should' be heterosexual. The acceptance of a particular partner, the desire for a particular touch or kiss or bodily penetration was affected as much by how those acts were classified as by the objective nature of the stimulation (1992: 241).

Whether they are now homosexual or heterosexual, transsexuals' histories reveal both constancy of the object of desire and, in a weak sense, their own psychosexual identities. I say 'in a weak sense' only to acknowledge their longstanding confusion and lack of confidence before their acceptance of that psychosexual identity.

A further insight into psychosexual identity that was foreshadowed in chapter two is the nature of reciprocity, that is, reciprocal sexual attraction between individuals. On several occasions transsexuals described instances of mistaken identity in the earliest stages of relationships with other people, a situation not unknown in transsexual circles (see Money 1988: 92). The type of situation was the same in each case although the gender of the partners varied. On one occasion, for example, a pre-operative transsexual described the early stages of what she thought was a developing relationship with a heterosexual man. That relationship came to an abrupt halt when he realised the person he was warming to was not an 'effeminate gay man' but a transsexual who saw herself as a heterosexual woman. Two important points emerge from this sort of situation. First, in developing sexual relationships, people are initially attracted to outward appearance or body morphology rather than biological sex determined by genitalia. Given that most social interaction takes place between clothed individuals, we do not routinely do genital checks to determine another's sex. This point is well put by Money (1988: 42) and Grimm (1987: 82–83) who both talk about the significance of body morphology in sexual attraction. Also, this point is consistent with the earlier discussion of doing gender in everyday life and the importance of key gender markers. In the case of mistaken identity above, initial attraction involved each partner attributing not merely gender to the other person, but also a more inclusive psychosexual identity, that is, 'heterosexual man' and 'effeminate, gay man'.

The second point is that, unlike the type of case above, when relationships do continue, reciprocated desire helps to confirm one's own psychosexual identity. In other words, if a transsexual sees herself as a heterosexual woman and is attracted to a man who desires and sees her in those terms, then her own psychosexual identity is confirmed and reinforced.[12] In such a relationship, there must be correspondence of self-identity and how one is seen by a partner for that relationship to continue. The breakdown of this correspondence was illustrated in those few cases mentioned earlier, of wives claiming they had reached the point where the marriage relationship could not continue because they felt like a 'lesbian' when involved in close physical, sexual contact.

These aspects of desire provide a link with the claim that transsexuals are not a third gender but largely conform to existing expectations of feminine women. In other words, in their sexual relationships, they see themselves, and their partners see them, first as women and then, more implicitly, as heterosexual women or lesbians. This pattern was universal among transsexuals in this study. There were no sexual revolutionaries. Whether heterosexual or lesbian, they all saw themselves as women; they stressed the importance of having a woman's body and looking like women, and of being regarded as women by their partners and the wider society. The patterns of desire, especially how transsexuals saw themselves and the nature of their own relationships, are illustrated in figure 5:4, where, for comparison, the picture of heterosexual and homosexual men and women is included. 'Transsexual' is a separate category in this figure only to indicate the separate patterns for the people in this study. What the figure is saying is that where a sexual relationship exists, it is viewed by self and partner to be one of four dominant types. Notwithstanding the varying social legitimacy attached to these relationships, they involve (a) heterosexual man and woman, (b) heterosexual woman and man, (c) homosexual men and (d) homosexual women. These four types of relationship are indicated by the four dark areas on the grid. They are dominant because virtually all sexual relationships fall into one of these categories at any one time.[13] Regardless of whether they were heterosexual or homosexual, transsexuals involved in a relationship saw it as one of these dominant types.

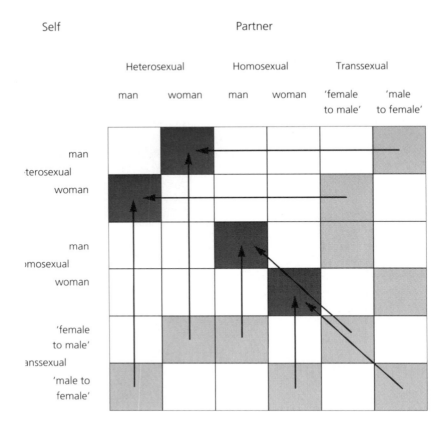

Figure 5:4 *Patterns of self-identity and sexual desire*

No transsexual saw herself or was seen by her partner as a 'transsexual'. Where, for example, a transsexual was involved in a relationship with a homosexual woman who was not a transsexual (middle light grey area in the bottom row), the relationship was viewed by both as a lesbian relationship (vertical arrow pointing towards the dark grey area in the fourth row). Although this study did not systematically examine the situation of female to male transsexuals, the light grey areas indicate all the logical possibilities one would expect to find among all transsexuals.

Wider research on transsexuals bears out these claims about how transsexuals see themselves and are seen by their partners. Green (1974: 67ff.) and Money (1988: 92), in discussing the partners of male to female transsexuals, make the point that even when a man knows his partner is a transsexual, his sexual emotional response acknowledges her as a woman although intellectually he may reflect on that situation in between times. Green (1974: 118) and Money (1988: 93) both make a similar point about partners of female to male transsexuals. Even in more marginal types of relationships there is evidence that a transsexual's partner sees her as a certain type of woman. Money notes one type of situation:

> there are some male partners of pre-operative male to female transsexuals who are strongly attracted to a lady with a penis as a sexuoerotic partner. Postsurgically, their attraction wanes, and the partnership dissolves (1988: 92).

The important aspect of transsexuals' relationships is the way their partners see them, that is, as women. It would be easy, however, to assume that they would have greater success in forming relationships than they actually do, a point that applies especially to heterosexuals, that is, male to female transsexuals attracted to men. Other research, such as that by Green (1974: 129) and Millot (1990: 106-107), is consistent with the picture of transsexuals in this study, among whom stable, enduring sexual relationships, especially with men, have been difficult to attain and retain.

Viewing transsexuals in their social context shows that their transsexualism is a response to the rigidity of the socially legitimate categories 'heterosexual man' and 'heterosexual woman'. In spite of the rigidity and the ethical strictures of this dichotomy, transsexuals are a manifestation of a range of psychosexual identities that, historically, has surfaced in different ways and, until recently, were looked upon as idiosyncratic. The most obvious illustrations are those males and females who have lived in the *other* gender out of psychological necessity, with Herculine Barbin

(Foucault 1980) and Eugenia Falleni (Falkiner 1988) being two of the more prominent illustrations. Examination of gender along-side desire reinforces the point that recognition by scholars of this range of psychosexual identities does not necessarily mean that gender is continuous. Williams, for instance, correctly notes that

> certain individuals clearly do not want to limit their sexuality by labels of 'gay' or 'straight'. Others do not want to fit into a tight box of defining themselves as 'men' or as 'women'. Sexuality and gender are closely related in this respect (1987: 136)

but he is making an assumption, like others such as Devor (1987; 1989), Freimuth and Hornstein (1982: 516, 527–528) and, possibly, Davies (1990: 501),[14] in the slide to saying that all this represents a move in a 'more gender blending direction' (1987: 136). Sexual desire and reciprocity among transsexuals and others are not random but specific, which suggests the existence of a number of categories or, at least, identifiable clusters of psycho-sexual identities or gender types.

Another advantage of linking gender with sexual desire is that it demonstrates that transsexuals are not a third gender but people who have a commitment to the ideal of feminine women and, for many transsexuals in this study, an avoidance of anything that smacks of aggressive, masculine men. What is more important is that linking gender and sexual desire exposes not only the unrealistic nature of the man–woman dichotomy but also is saying something about persistence of the wider, socially prescribed dichotomy of heterosexual men and women. Despite an immense literature that has critically focused on that dichotomy, only some of which has been used elsewhere in this book,[15] it persists.[16] Further, in the face of so much social evidence to the contrary, there is embedded in that dichotomy an assumption that 'biology is destiny'. This assumption is succinctly captured by Justice Kirby (1988: vii–viii) in his criticism of Ormrod's judgement in the legal case in which Corbett challenged the validity of his marriage to the well-known transsexual April Ashley. Kirby notes:

since marriage postulates a relationship between a man and a woman, if Miss Ashley was not a woman, the 'marriage' was a nullity ... There was no statute governing the case ... no clearly applicable judicial precedent ... The judge ... could have assigned primacy to the social and sexual objectives of marriage. Instead, he preferred ... to adopt three criteria to determine April Ashley's sex assignment: chromosomal, gonadal and genital ... Thus, instead of looking at marriage in a modern context as a social contract ... between two adults permitting them to live together, have sexual relations, and no less a marriage than many others because no children could result, Ormrod J preferred scientific criteria. In the face of the chromosomal test, all the external social indicia of a human relationship fell away, melted by the discovery of a genetic pattern, marked before birth, but demonstrable only by peering down a microscope.

This case is important because Ormrod's judgement straddles the 'biology is destiny' assumption in the heterosexual man–woman dichotomy evident in both scholarly and everyday circles. It is difficult simply to argue that certain beliefs about biology maintain the social manifestations of that dichotomy. What then is and has been the driving force behind its maintenance? This is a question that will also be taken up in the next chapter.

The persistence of the heterosexual man–woman dichotomy with its strong 'biology is destiny' assumption suggests continuing uncertainty in scholarly circles about the origins of gender. Highly explanatory theories have great attraction in a milieu of uncertainty. Early uncertainty about gays and lesbians, for instance, saw them being viewed as a third sex (Buchbinder 1994: 57). Transsexuals being similarly regarded suggests similar uncertainty about their existence and increasing visibility. This uncertainty, arguably, extends beyond the academic realm into humour. Szasz's cynical metaphor about 'transchronologism' (see note 16) has an equal in Jim Davis's *Garfield* (see overleaf).

GARFIELD   **by Jim Davis**

Finally, it is worth noting that Williams views gender as 'an ongoing *process*' (1987: 137, his emphasis) involving the interaction of biological and social factors. This is an important point because it not only corresponds to the evidence presented in this chapter, but also foreshadows the discussion in the next chapter of what I call the analysis of hope in relation to the social factors maintaining the current rigid gender dichotomy.

NOTES

1 In the scholarly literature there are a few authors who claim, or refer to those who claim, that transsexuals are a 'third gender' or 'third sex'; see, for example, Ross (1986a: 5); Wikan (1977); Goodman (1983); Kessler and McKenna (1985); and Millot (1990: 129-130).

2 Notwithstanding the inappropriateness of the term 'passing', a discussion of this concept from an ethnomethodological perspective is contained in the journal *Gender and Society* (1992: 169-214).

3 At a more macro level the taken for grantedness of individuals' ways of apprehending the world or their patterned consciousness is an important aspect of recent approaches to the study of culture. Methodologically it is important because, when interviewing, it is not simply a matter of asking subjects what they believe and what they stand for, see Jackson (1989) and Lewins (1992b).

4 Given that some of these comments by professionals were made as early as the mid-1970s, the use of the word 'feminine' was unreflective and almost synonymous with 'woman'.

5 See also Kessler's (1990) later work on the medical management of intersexed infants, the article 'The medical construction of gender: case management of intersexed infants'. Contrary to what the title might suggest, this paper provides another insight on gender as a managed accomplishment.

6 This observation corresponds with Green's (1974: 120) finding that pre-operative transsexuals do not want their genitals manipulated because it interferes with their self-concept as women.

7 Synnott (1989) provides useful insights on the significance of hair for males and females. His notion of opposite sexes having opposite hair—that is, long for females and short for males—applies to male to female and female to male transsexuals, for whom hair assumes immense importance, especially if facial hair is included. Green (1974: 102) makes a similar point about male to female and female to male transsexuals being mirror images of each other. For a wider discussion of the significance of other parts of the body, see Synnott (1993).

8 The previous chapter noted the sense of urgency among younger transsexuals to have reassignment surgery. Controlling for age in both categories—that is, younger and older transsexuals—those with the lowest levels of education and manual occupations had the strongest desire for surgery, as well as being those who most wanted breast

augmentation surgery and a sexual relationship with a heterosexual man.

9 The title of King's (1993) book (*The Transvestite and the Transsexual: Public Categories and Private Identities*) conveys a similar point about the tension between the public and private aspects of transsexuals' psychosexual identities. The diverse and historical nature of psycho-sexual identities is receiving increasing attention from male scholars outside 'women's studies' circles; see, for example, Halperin (1990) and Buchbinder (1994).

10 This position is close to King's (1984: 48-50; 1993) 'role model'. See also Connell (1983: 21).

11 This claim corresponds with Tully's (1992: 58) observation of male to female transsexuals.

12 Tully (1992: 242) draws the same relationship between a transsex-ual's identity and the nature of reciprocity with a sexual partner when he says that 'their [transsexuals'] gender style shift carried identity with it, as they sought the reciprocal sexual response they desired'. Money (1988: 81) makes a similar point about the role of reciprocity in boys who became homosexual in adulthood. As he says, 'reinforcement of what matured into homosexual eroticism began rather as an endorsement of gender cross coding, possibly related to sensuous closeness and affectionate closeness with a male'. Similarly, Archer and Lloyd (1987: 120) make the point that desire assists categorisation in the case of homosexuals.

13 I say 'at any one time' because even a bisexual man, for example, with any one partner, sees himself as a man and expects his partner to do likewise. There are of course sexual desires involving more marginalised people such as pedophiles. Disregarding the legal and human rights issues surrounding such relationships, most can be fitted into the matrix in figure 5:4 by allowing for partners' ages. This need for a more diverse range of psychosexual categories is not new and has been at least implicitly foreshadowed in the literature; see for example Money's concepts of 'identification and complemen-tation' (1988: 71ff.) and Grimm's concepts of 'complementarity and similarity' (1987: 79-85).

14 I say 'possibly' in the case of Davies because it is difficult to say that she assumes a continuous notion of gender as her view is future oriented. She notes,

> our patterns of desire are organized around and in terms of
> our gendered identity ... I desire a world in which there are

multiple ways of being that are available to everyone, that multiplicity not being organized around the male/female dualism (1990: 501).

15 See, for example, Rubin (1975), Grimm (1987), Raymond (1979), D'Emilio (1983), and Buchbinder (1994).

16 Arguably, the persistence of this dichotomy is evident in the vantage point of some scholars who trivialise transsexualism. Note, for example, the following comment from an article in *Time* some years ago:

> when 'transsexualism', or discomfort about one's anatomic gender and the desire to change, was made an official disorder, psychiatrist Thomas Szasz derisively claimed to be suffering from 'transchronologism' because he was dissatisfied with his current age and wanted to be younger (Leo 1985: 68).

If one took this sort of comment by Szasz seriously, then it would be necessary to come to grips with people who wanted a species change. This, in turn, raises the question of how would one cope, for example, with the main character in the well-known film *Birdie*? This film is about a man who believes he is a bird and his attempts to live as one. Perhaps more outrageously, would we have to take seriously animals who act out of character, such as dogs who appear to mimic cats?

6
Conclusion

The evidence presented in chapters four and five shows that for male to female transsexuals in this study becoming a woman is a process. By examining the nature of their social contexts, the macro and micro dimensions of that process reveal considerable variation among those individuals. At a micro level, for example, some transsexuals learn better than others the significance and skills of doing gender. Also, educational and occupational backgrounds are closely associated with different responses to the body, with the less educated invoking a wider social discourse that stresses the significance of the genitals in characterising gender. By contrast, educated professionals stress a personal discourse that is more pragmatic and focused on the significance of key gender markers, such as long hair, the absence of facial hair, and signs of breast development. Despite this internal variation among transsexuals, all revealed a deep structural similarity in the necessity for the body and one's gender to correspond. Such correspondence is to a conventional image of feminine women, which negates the idea that they are sexual revolutionaries and a third gender. Plato may have written about three sexes—males, females and androgynes—in his *Symposium* (Goodman 1983: 216), but all the historical and contemporary evidence suggests that transsexualism does not represent a third sex or gender but rather the response to 'gender dimorphism on the part of society' (Grimm 1987: 81).[1]

More specifically, transsexualism is a response to the rigid, socially prescribed gender dichotomy of heterosexual men and women. I add 'heterosexual' to indicate the value of viewing gender in relation to sexual desire. This has provided not only a clarification of the ways transsexuals negotiate their past and current personal relations, but also points to the nature of the determinist, gendered world we all live in and the sorts of strains it is experiencing. The growing visibility of gay and lesbian political activity and increasing evidence that previous estimates of the incidence of transsexualism are not merely too low, but meaningless, indicate a variety of psychosexual identities confronting an extremely rigid gender dichotomy. We may be 'on the verge of a Kuhnian revolution in terms of understanding how gender is socially constructed' (Grimm 1987: 84) but caution is warranted when it comes to accepting some views on (a) the nature and construction of gender, (b) the 'big picture' concerning *how* transsexualism is socially constructed and (c) how transsexuals should position themselves politically in today's society.

These issues are interrelated and, because they require further clarification, will be examined separately below. This examination will also clarify some of the residual questions not answered or addressed in earlier chapters. The question of what explains gender if it is not sex differences was raised in chapter two. This was in response to Garber's (1993) view that the social reality of gender difference begets a recourse to biological sex differences to explain gender. This and the question foreshadowed in chapter five of why the rigid heterosexual man–woman dichotomy persists will be examined in considering (a) above. Also, the question of why there is a predominance of male to female transsexuals will be addressed in considering (b). In addition, I briefly return to the empirical evidence collected from transsexuals to comment on the long term picture for post-operative transsexuals. This book concludes with my own personal comments speaking as a parent of a transsexual.

Finally, I should make explicit two particular topics I have not addressed. The first is transsexualism and the law. This vast area includes issues such as the legality of changing the sex on transsexuals' birth certificates; equal opportunity guarantees in the workplace; protection under anti-discrimination legislation; the legal control of reassignment surgery; recognition of reassignment in criminal law; and human rights, including the right to marry. I have not addressed these issues because either they have been covered by others, such as Finlay (1988), or I do not have the legal competence to do them justice. The other topic I have not touched on, at least in any detail, is the ethical significance of transsexualism, especially reassignment surgery. This discussion forms a part of a forthcoming book on ethical issues in which I examine a number of ethical issues in their social contexts.

The Nature and Construction of Gender

As noted earlier, Garber's (1993) claim that gender is causally prior to biological sex differences leaves us with the problem of explaining gender, especially the persistence of the rigid hetero-sexual man–woman dichotomy. This problem is not fully dealt with in the literature on gender and, because of the possibility of mistaken theorising about the links between biology and gender, it is worth looking more closely at this relationship.

Garber is not alone in suggesting that biology has no causal influence on gender, for Kessler and McKenna (1985) make a similar claim. The mistaken theorising surrounding the link between biology and gender is that the theory Garber adopts must be right because the only other view is that biology determines gender and that is clearly wrong, as evidenced by the existence of transsexuals. The mistake in this sort of theorising is assuming that biology has either *no* influence on gender or that it determines gender.

Extending this mistaken theorising, if one accepts that gender causes the invoking of biological sex differences, which in turn are used to explain gender, then it is easy to see how one could claim that the 'biology causes gender' model is similar to 'racism', where social attributes (for example, poverty, alcoholism) are 'explained' by biological attributes: 'It is because they are black that they are poor and alcoholics'! The comparison between gender and race is not that unusual because, as Hausman points out,

> gender ... is an emphatically *social* category, similar to race and class in its dependence on ideological regulation and equivalent to them insofar as each contributes to the construction of subjectivity (1992: 273, her emphasis).

If one accepts that the invalid causal connection between biology and social attributes constitutes racism, then, strictly speaking, it follows that the explanation of the gender dichotomy by an appeal to biological sex differences would be 'sexism'.

I am not suggesting that Garber and Kessler and McKenna hold this view but their lack of focus on the origins of gender, especially its historical roots, makes one wonder. The purpose of this discussion, however, is not to launch a critique of these authors. Rather, I want to demonstrate that, in rejecting the model that sex differences cause gender, one does not *have* to accept the reverse argument that Garber proposes, and one does not have to accept the position that sex differences have played *no* role in shaping the heterosexual man–woman dichotomy.

If one were to accept that sex differences are not the cause but rather the effects of a gendered world, then one would also accept the comparison with racism above, where an invalid causal connection is drawn between observable social attributes and biology. Scholars in the ethnic and race relations area make the point that the symbolic significance historically attached to skin colour has been a consequence of the power of whites, generally, in their colonisation and domination of blacks. This means that skin colour could have been replaced by any other easily discerned physical marker capable of differentiation.

To appreciate this point, it is worth diverting for a moment to consider a hypothetical race relations situation in which the symbolic significance is reversed, that is, where black skinned people's dominance over whites is a taken for granted, stable state. This hypothetical picture achieves three purposes.

1 The skin colour reversal helps us see the processes that surround something arbitrary like skin colour and its relationship to a form of social differentiation of immense significance.

2 In equating racism with sexism, it allows for the ready substitution of one biological difference for another, that is, 'female' in place of 'white skin' and 'male' in place of 'black skin'. It also allows for a corresponding substitution of social attributes, social expectations and behaviours of women in place of those for whites, and a corresponding switch of the expectations and behaviours associated with men in place of those for blacks.

3 It is possible to see in this situation a comparison with transsexuals who undergo reassignment surgery to give them an approximation of the biological attributes of females. This is not an issue I want to develop or to put too fine a point on. I

merely want to identify three points of comparison: (a) the similarity of the often shared, symbolic significance of skin colour among blacks and whites and the deep structure of the importance of the body corresponding with one's gender; (b) the difficulty of breaking the perceived nexus between biological and social attributes, whether it be at the level of thought or political action; and (c) the way in which biology is equated with nature and then used as an ethical yardstick to evaluate change in behaviour. From this hypothetical situation the question of whether sexism is comparable with racism will provide a way of evaluating Garber's argument about the priority of gender.

A metaphor—the black and white nature of being black and white

Imagine a society in which skin colour is the most significant basis of social differentiation. People with black skin have political control and almost all the valued resources, such as wealth, income and prestige, whereas citizens with white skin, despite being roughly half the population, have little access to those resources. Further, imagine that over a period of centuries, this pattern remains constant with blacks generally receiving the highest levels of education, the best jobs and the highest incomes. Leading elegant lives in sumptuous homes, they view their achievements and their dominant role in society as the consequence of their natural superiority. After all, they hold, blacks would not be where they are if they did not have a predilection to rule, a greater strength of moral character, and a civilised nature. By contrast, whites have always been in the worst jobs, lived in the worst areas in substandard housing in which they barely survive. They are regarded by blacks as dirty, ignorant, rude and clearly not deserving anything better. Even if good housing and so on were given to whites, blacks argue, they would not appreciate their value. In a society with no intermarriage, the difference between black and white is very black and white. To be black is to be superior: even whites will confirm this axiom.

Everyday patterns of relations between blacks and whites are taken for granted, so much so that both categories hardly ever give the nature of their different situations a thought. Why should they? After all, everyone is told in church that it is natural or God given that things should be the way they are. Everyone has a place and everyone knows their place. At least this pattern is the public facade, for there are some whites who privately express their resentment of the way they are pushed around and denied access to society's rewards. Why should being white prevent them from competing with blacks in the same social arena? After all, they suggest, being black does not naturally give them the right to define what whites should and should not aspire to. Blacks, on learning of these lone voices through public graffiti and anonymous pamphlets, are astounded. How, they exclaim, can whites be so outrageous? It is perfectly plain for anyone to see that to be black is to be superior and civilised: to be white is to be inferior and in need of the sort of guidance blacks provide. To challenge this is like saying that pigs ought to be able to fly if they want to.

Despite the longstanding habit of blacks punishing whites who do not show proper deference and who do not acknowledge their true station in life, there are whites who have been exposed for darkening their skin and attempting to live as blacks. Some of these people, with considerable personal cost in terms of personal anxiety and money, have even had their skin permanently dyed black. This practice is the subject of considerable media attention and an issue that leads many blacks to ask publicly, 'How many whites are there posing as blacks and gaining access to that which is not rightfully theirs? Once a white always a white!'

Now, after a few decades of public visibility of the practice of whites attempting to live as blacks by darkening their skin, there are some unexpected developments. There are some blacks, mainly educated professionals, who support whites who want to change their skin colour. Extraordinarily, there are even a few blacks who want to change their skin colour to white. Further, there are people who for years have been accepted as 'model black citizens' only to be exposed in the media as being 'really' white. Not surprisingly, there is considerable confusion, among both blacks and whites. Public discussion attempts to clarify the issues. Blacks ask 'What's so wrong with being born white?' They answer their own question by asserting that if skin colour is natural then it is wrong to change it. Many whites who have changed or are contemplating changing their skin colour point out the necessity of the colour transition. All without exception accept that it is totally unthinkable not to have black skin if you are going to live the way blacks do. But there is also a tiny minority who are raising even more provocative questions. They ask, for example, whether it is an assumption that a black way of life automatically follows from being black. Might lifestyle have little or nothing to do with skin colour? Others are asking why is it necessary for people who want to live as blacks to go through the complex and costly process of changing skin colour. What is it in our society that prevents them from just living that way?

What then does this lengthy metaphor tell us? Can we say that sexism fits the mould provided by this example of racism? The short answer is 'not exactly'. As previously noted, skin colour in this sort of situation is somewhat arbitrary in that there is no necessary link between skin colour and the social attributes that are said to emanate from that biological 'fact'. In the case of biological sex differences, however, there *is* a link to the social attributes surrounding being either a heterosexual man or woman. That link is the abiding reality of sexed bodies capable of reproduction. This link warrants some elaboration.

Given that most children, historically, have been born into families, the reality of reproduction goes a long way towards explaining why the heterosexual man–woman dichotomy persists. This is represented diagramatically in figure 6:1. It indicates that it is not merely the existence of family life as the locus of reproduction that has created and maintained the rigidity of the gender dichotomy. Before the emergence of large cities and industrialisation, families in an agricultural mode of production were generally more conscious of the link between their labour and survival. In the background, the absence of children might have meant a break in the family line but also, in the foreground, it meant the absence of labour essential for survival. The historical significance of the value of having sons rather than daughters can be linked to this predicament. Furthermore, the arrangements surrounding reproduction were only patterned because they needed to be controlled. Arguably, the closer a community was to the margins of survival, the greater the social controls surrounding reproduction. Those controls included the enshrining of legitimate reproduction in law in the form of marriage;[2] the emergence of incest rules; strong sanctions against adultery and the absence of virginity; and, possibly, rules of inheritance. Also, there has been the more informal control of infanticide of females.

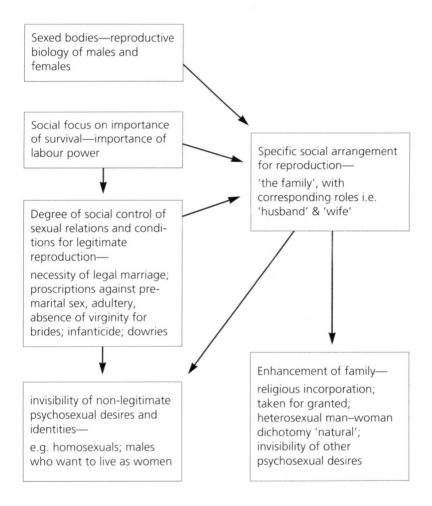

Figure 6:1 *Factors creating and maintaining the heterosexual man–woman dichotomy*

From the reality of the family as the locus of reproduction have emerged the social factors creating and maintaining the taken for grantedness of the heterosexual man–woman dichotomy. This is not to say that a variety of psychosexual identities have not always existed. Chapter two provided evidence of a long history of transsexualism in all societies.[3] Until recently the social reality in many societies has been one in which non-legitimate psychosexual identities, such as homosexuality and males who want to live as women, have been invisible because of explicit social control ranging from stigma to stoning.[4] The final factor in this picture is that, historically, it has been males who have exercised greater control over arrangements surrounding sexual relations.

It is not as if anything I have said above is new. Scholars such as Archer (1987: 87), Gatens (1983: 148, 156) and Turner (1991: 20), for example, have stressed the importance of different bodies and reproduction when theorising gender relations. Others have pointed to the role of the family and reproduction in relation to survival. Gough (1975: 74), for instance, stresses the importance of the sexual division of labour in the family as being 'crucial for food production'. Also, Money and Tucker (1977: 76) implicitly point to the historical importance of fertility for survival when they claim that, in assigning sex among children with ambiguous sexual characteristics, the push for arbitrary reassignment is usually based on 'the importance of preserving presumed fertility'. Capturing the historical importance of reproduction, the academic lawyer Finlay (1988: 56) quotes Justice Ormrod's judgement on the issue of the legality of April Ashley's marriage. Ormrod, in referring to submissions that 'confuse sex with gender', posits that 'marriage is a relationship which depends on sex and not on gender'. In terms of social control, it is no accident that Turner (1984) should link reproduction with patriarchy in his analysis of the four tasks with which bodies confront social organisations (see also Frank 1990: 131-162).

Life, however, is no longer 'a lumbering process' in the negotiation of survival: it is 'not simply birth, growth and death' (Singer 1977: 51). The current reality is an increasing separation of reproduction from psychosexual identity (see D'Emilio 1983: 143), largely because of the declining necessity of the family for survival, which in turn has lessened the circumstances maintaining the taken for grantedness of the heterosexual man–woman dichotomy. This change is indicated by an increasing number of people not marrying; an increasing number of married people not having children; an increasing visibility of hitherto non legitimate psychosexual identities, such as homosexuals and transsexuals; and the possibility of male homosexuals and male to female transsexuals seeking the medical implantation of a fertilised egg into their abdomen leading to 'a male "pregnancy" ' (Finlay and Walters 1988: xv–xvi).

We may say, then, that in rejecting the model that sex differences cause gender, one does not *have* to accept the reverse argument that Garber proposes. Nor does one have to accept the position that sex differences have played *no* role in shaping the heterosexual man–woman dichotomy. Connell (1987: 66) is correct in criticising the assumption in 'our culture' that 'the reproductive dichotomy is ... the absolute basis of gender and sexuality in everyday life'. Leaving gender and sexuality or psychosexual variation unexplained, however, whether one accepts Garber's model or not, is counter-empirical and ahistorical (see Gatens 1983: 144) alongside the evidence showing *a* role for biology in determination and maintenance of the heterosexual man–woman dichotomy. In saying that the latter is only one manifestation of the full range of psychosexual identities is another way of saying that the role biology has played is limited. Hopefully, however, my desire for precision here has not merged into tediousness. Whether or not, given the gaps in some approaches to the broad area of gender studies, precision is certainly warranted.

These gaps, resulting from evidence having been overlooked and reliance on assertions, are similar to faults in some accounts of the social construction of transsexualism.

The Big Picture on the Construction of Transsexualism

I use the term 'big picture' to characterise those attempts to explain transsexualism by analysing the phenomenon at the level of whole societies. By standing back far enough from the event to be explained, in this case transsexualism, it is possible to produce simple, highly explanatory theories. Raymond is the most well-known researcher to adopt this sort of theory. As she puts it:

> the First Cause, that which sets other causes of transsexualism in motion ... is a patriarchal society, which generates norms of masculinity and femininity. Uniquely restricted by patriarchy's definitions of masculinity and femininity, the transsexual becomes body-bound by them and merely rejects one and gravitates toward the other (1979: 70).

In such a society, 'patriarchy is molding and mutilating *male* flesh, but for the purpose of *constructing women*'. Transsexualism 'may be one way by which men attempt to possess females' creative energies, by possessing artifactual female organs' (Raymond 1979: xvi, her emphasis). What are we to make of this sort of argument? King (1993; 1984) includes it as well in his 'false consciousness model', as do Billings and Urban (1982) and Sagarin (1978). Disregarding her use of 'may', which also implies 'may not', the use of abstract concepts such as 'patriarchy' provide an easy recourse to a simple explanation, but at the societal level she does not provide adequate evidence of patriarchy. There is no evidence of a reified patriarchal society doing anything. This is not surprising because concepts like 'society' are not concrete things and, therefore, do not do anything. The 'doing of things' is confined to people in the social realm. A similar resort to a simple, abstract argument lacking adequate evidence is her claim that within a patriarchal society there is a 'medical empire' in which medical specialities have combined 'to create transsexuals' (1979: xv). I do not deny the role of medical technology here, for without it no amount of subjectivity and conviction could produce the results reassignment surgery provides (see Hausman 1992: 300; Millot 1990: 142; and Collyer 1994).[5] Raymond's abstract theory premised on patriarchal society, however, lacks evidence and suggests uncertainty on her part. Uncertainty is replaced by the 'certainty' of a highly explanatory theory that is difficult to test.

Using this approach, Raymond seeks to explain the preponderance of male to female transsexuals, a situation foreshadowed earlier. She attempts to explain this at an equally abstract level by making the highly speculative claim that it results from men recognising the power of women by virtue of their biology and power in giving birth (1979: xv-xvi). All this is counter-empirical because it overlooks:

(a) the growing proportion of visible female to male transsexuals. Raymond, admittedly writing in the late 1970s when female to male transsexuals were less visible, brushes aside this point by viewing them as the '*token* that saves the face for the male "transsexual empire"' (1979: 27, her emphasis);

(b) transsexuals' life long history of gender dysphoria. If Raymond seriously believes that male to female transsexualism has anything to do with men recognising the power of women, then she is imputing motives and a level of consciousness infant children could not possibly have; and

(c) transsexuals' lack of political consciousness and involvement. To the extent that male to female transsexuals are male, they are, in Raymond's view, a part of the male conspiracy along with male doctors or, as Millot (1990: 13) says in characterising Raymond's stance, 'transsexuality is the latest male ploy designed to ensure man's continuing ascendancy in the battle of the sexes'. Most transsexuals, however, want invisibility and do not organise as transsexuals or declare their backgrounds (see Harding 1986: 115). By contrast, some transsexuals who are politicised are not drawing on any attributes of 'women' but are challenging the conventional masculine and feminine identities of men and women.

If Raymond's explanation of the preponderance of male to female transsexuals is lacking, then what explains this preponderance? Garber provides no explanation but observes

> the public's fascination with men who have been surgically transformed to women when they are alive, and with women who have lived their whole lives as men, only after they are *dead*. This cultural fascination with women as *either* dead *or* culturally constructed, already artifactual, is a tradition in Western literature and art at least as old as Petrarch (1993: 110, her emphasis).

Green (1974: 101) posits a variety of reasons for the greater visibility of male to female transsexuals:

(a) there is a likelihood of errors in the psychosexual development of males as a consequence of the masculinising role of gonadal hormone;

(b) at the social level there is more latitude allowed to females in their pursuit of cross gender roles, a point also made by Stuart (1983:32);

(c) the first person everyone identifies with is their mother and any subsequent shift of identity is required only of males; and

(d) the reassignment surgery for female to male transsexuals is more difficult.

Hausman (1992: 299) echoes the latter reason along with the claim that, historically, gender clinics have existed for male to female transsexuals and have catered to their needs. This 'catering to male desire' argument is inconclusive because it poses a 'chicken–egg' problem. Did the clinics emerge because of the presence of transsexuals with particular needs or did male to female transsexuals emerge in greater numbers because of the establishment of clinics suited to their needs? This question raises the distinction between factors behind the origin of an event and those that maintain it. They are not always identical. Given the political and ethical sensitivities surrounding reassignment surgery, clinics did not emerge before the visibility of transsexuals with particular needs. Once a going concern, though, the ease of obtaining surgery, as Walters (1988: 27) notes, will influence the number presenting at a clinic. On balance, I believe there are many reasons for the greater visibility of male to female transsexuals, some of which are touched on above. There is, however, a lot we do not know about female to male transsexuals. It is simply too easy to assume that they are 'mirror images' (Green 1974: 102) or 'opposite' (see Synnott 1989) of male to female transsexuals. We do not fully understand the extent of totally different patterns and processes among female to male transsexuals, a topic that is worthy of another book.

Political Implications

Another area we know little about is the range of political orientations among male to female transsexuals, that is, the extent to which they are involved in attempting to change wider social responses to transsexualism. At one level there are those who identify themselves as 'women' and value conventional images of femininity.[6] I believe the majority of this category wish to become socially invisible and remain politically uninvolved in terms of issues concerning transsexuals. For the people in this study, this was the final stage in the macro process of becoming a woman. At this same level a minority are politically involved and have publicly declared their transsexual background in an endeavour to bring about reforms, such as allowing change of one's sex on a birth certificate, anti-discrimination legislation and human rights guarantees.

At another level, there are those transsexuals who challenge the rigidity of the conventional categories 'masculine man' and 'feminine woman' by adopting a radical approach to their own gender and, in some cases, to gender in society. Gender is viewed in a number of ways, as 'lifestyle', 'a performance' and/or as 'ways of being'. It is this dimension of political challenge to the existing gender dichotomy, as Connell (1987: 76) notes in referring to the work of Roberta Perkins (1983), that makes the whole area of transsexualism more complex. Within this level, there is a similar separation of those transsexuals who are political involved and those not involved. Figure 6:2 indicates the logical possibilities in

Psychosexual identity	Degree of political involvement	
	Involved	Non-involved
Sees self/own gender as feminine 'woman' (conservative)		
Sees self/own gender in one of a variety of ways of being— e.g. 'transsexual' (radical)		

Figure 6:2 *Political orientations of transsexuals*

terms of what I prefer to call psychosexual identity and degree of political involvement.

In short, coexisting with politically involved and non-involved transsexuals, who are conventional in terms of the existing gender dichotomy (the top row of figure 6:2), are those who see or identify themselves in a variety of ways. As Connell (1987: 76) notes, in the subcultures of prostitution and show business this includes seeing oneself as a 'transsexual' rather than as a 'man' or 'woman'. This level (bottom row of figure 6:2) includes the politically involved and uninvolved, the latter implicitly identified by Connell (1987: 76), who characterises them as 'uncertain about where they belong and why'. So, in attempting to gain a broad view of transsexuals, it is not a case of either–or, that is, whether transsexuals are conventional or whether they challenge existing gender categories. Although transsexuals in this study all fall into the top row of figure 6:2, and therefore reinforce the existing gender dichotomy, this is not to say that all transsexuals are similarly located.

One implication of accepting this range of transsexuals in terms of their identities and political involvement is that it exposes a weakness in some academic work on transsexualism. The analysis of hope was foreshadowed in the previous chapter where I suggested that some scholars seemed to blame transsexuals for adopting conventional approaches to gender and having to resort to reassignment surgery to alleviate their anxiety. Singer (1977: 52) conveys this blame when she comments on the significance of Jan Morris becoming a woman:

the whole point is lost, it seems to me, when people become obsessed with the idea that they have to prove to the world, by making *visible* changes in themselves, that they have undergone a process of psychological adaptation. If, as it has now come to be accepted generally, each person has a variety of psychological tendencies and capabilities that fall into both 'masculine' and 'feminine' categories, then the question, 'Which is predominant?' is the wrong question. What needs to be asked is, 'How are these aspects within myself relating to each other?' If peace about this is established within the individual, there will be no need for public proclamation [her emphasis].

Similarly, Raymond (1979: 176) poses the question

> isn't it possible for persons who desire sex conversion surgery, and who have also experienced sex role oppression and dissatisfaction with their bodies, to band together around their own unique form of gender agony—especially those who claim to have a deep commitment to feminism?

I quote Singer and Raymond at length because they and others, such as Devor (1987; 1989), Grimm (1987: 68) and Greer (1986; 1989), seem to think that transsexuals only need to acknowledge what they are and choose a lifestyle commensurate with their psychosexual identity. As Singer's last sentence seems to suggest, it is lack of recognition of deep structure surrounding psychosexual identity and the body that possibly explains why this sort of analysis is based on hope rather than reality. 'If' is the key word: of course there is no need *if* individuals have peace. It is because the vast majority of transsexuals do not or cannot see their situation in any other way that poses the political and theoretical problem. In other words, whether our perspective on transsexualism is with a view to political intervention or intellectual understanding, we are historically and culturally located in a social reality that is a going concern. To suggest that there is no *need* for a gender dichotomy, or to ask why does it *have* to exist, is to opt for hope as a way of understanding rather than coming to grips with the difficult task of analysing what *is* the case.

It is not surprising that those who adopt a position based on hope should oppose reassignment surgery, as illustrated by Singer's (1977) comments above. The issue of surgery is the Achilles heel of that stance. Until we reach the stage when transsexuals no longer have the conviction of the need for reassignment surgery, which is a powerful statement about the sort of society in which they are located, what are they to do? My own view is that the perceived need for reassignment surgery is a stage in a wider social process that is still somewhat unclear. Social acceptance of what appears today to be an extreme position—that is, Grimm's (1987) notion of a 'woman with a penis'—would render reassignment surgery unnecessary. Perhaps the appropriate historical metaphor would be to liken acceptance of the 'woman with a penis' to acceptance of left-handedness as another 'way of being'. It is no longer 'necessary' or desirable to correct it. That moment in time, however, is not upon us.

Finally, in terms of the politics of transsexualism, there are those at the other extreme who believe that reassignment surgery should be freely available in what should be a client–provider relationship (see Collyer 1994). Although there is much in this argument I sympathise with, I believe it overlooks the politics surrounding reassignment surgery, both within the Australian medical profession and in the wider society. As Collyer (1994) herself notes, that sort of surgery is not high status professional activity and, at the Monash Medical Centre, along with other activities such as in-vitro fertilisation, it is not high on the list of priorities when it comes to governments spending the medical dollar! The reality is that for a variety of political reasons the Australian medical profession is forced to act conservatively when it comes to a client-driven approach to reassignment surgery.

The Long Term Picture

Given the strain of coping in a dichotomous gendered world, the question foreshadowed earlier, whether we should expect post-operative transsexuals to be paragons of mental health (Green and Fleming 1990: 173), brings us to the issue of the long term picture, especially where reassignment surgery is involved. Is reassignment surgery successful?

In any long term follow-up of transsexuals it is necessary to specify the criteria by which success is measured and what constitutes 'long term'. In Snaith *et al.*'s (1993) survey, the interval between surgery and evaluation was around five years. The criteria for assessment were 'partly based on a broad quality-of-life statement of "happiness", as well as satisfaction with the gender role reversal' (1993: 682). Their findings were:

(a) the majority of transsexuals experience a successful outcome 'in terms of subjective well being and personal happiness' (1993: 684);

(b) most female to male transsexuals 'were generally happier'

(1993: 682); and

(c) the experience of 'probably most' is 'loss of family and other relationships, of work, and of the esteem of others' (1993: 682).

Follow-up studies both here and overseas corroborate Walters' claim that 'the general consensus of opinion around the world' is that 'gender reassignment is, on balance, more effective than any other treatment for this condition'. He points to the Australian follow-up study that showed that 80 per cent of transsexuals after seven and a half years achieved a satisfactory result based on personal well being (1986: 131; 1988: 33-34; see also Walters, Kennedy and Ross 1986). This picture broadly corresponds with findings overseas.[7]

A comment on this picture is warranted, for the observation that female to male transsexuals do better in the long term is not an isolated claim. Money (1988: 92) and Abramowitz (1986: 188) make the same point with the latter mentioning 'several' researchers having reached the same conclusion. What is of particular interest is Abramowitz's acknowledgement that future research is needed to account for this phenomenon but that

> part of the answer may lie in the ... surgical advances and relatively benign resocialization norms for females to males (1986: 188).

Given that surgery is said to have a definite impact on body image and satisfaction for both male to female and female to male transsexuals (Lindgren and Pauly 1975; Fleming *et al.* 1982) and that, according to Green and Fleming (1990: 172), 'surgical adequacy' is a major factor in determining a favourable outcome, further long term follow-ups of transsexuals in Australia need to focus very carefully on the effects, as well as transsexuals' perceptions, of surgery.

Finally, the post-operative transsexuals in this study provide only limited insight into the long term picture. This is because it is difficult to know just how representative their current circumstances are in relation to those of all post-operative cases from the

Gender Dysphoria Clinic at the Monash Medical Centre and, indeed, all transsexuals in Australia. As indicated in chapter one, there are a number of differences when the transsexuals in this study are compared with all post-operative cases at the Clinic. It may be the case that greater cooperativeness on the part of those transsexuals I interviewed is a facet of their successful reassignment surgery and subsequent adjustment to living as women. This would appear to be the case if the recent survey of transsexuals in Sydney is taken as a comparison. Funded by the Australian Federation of Australian AIDS Organisations and the Commonwealth Department of Human Services and Health, that survey found alarmingly high levels of ill health, experience of discrimination and violence among the 146 transsexuals surveyed. As almost half were involved in sex work, however, the problem of representativeness looms again (Perkins *et al.* 1994; Harvey 1994).

With caution in mind concerning representativeness, some observations of post-operative transsexuals in this study are worth noting. Among the twenty individuals concerned, who comprised a little more than a third of those interviewed, almost half were in professional occupations or were self-employed. Twenty per cent were students and the same percentage in clerical and other occupations. Only 15 per cent were unemployed. In terms of the recency of surgical reassignment, 85 per cent had surgery less than five years before the time of interview. Compared to the picture gained from their case histories, all seemed well adjusted and positive about the future. Twenty per cent, that is four individuals, had some concern about the adequacy of their surgery. Two felt that the problem with their surgery was more than a minor, easily remedied matter. Obviously, from this limited number of relatively recent, surgically reassigned transsexuals it is not possible to say a great deal about the *long term* picture. A more systematic study among a larger and broader sample is warranted so that a clear picture of transsexuals' lives up to twenty years after surgery is possible. This comment is based not only on the nature of the sub-sample above, but also the complaint I heard from several transsexuals that there is a need for long term counselling, especially to deal with their difficulties in the areas of work and family.

A Parent's View

The preceding chapters are my attempt at a sociological analysis of transsexualism. Before I conclude, however, I want to make a brief comment as a parent of a post-operative transsexual. I do so partly because it is important to know the vantage point of the researcher in evaluating any attempt at sociological analysis, but mainly because some glimpse of my personal experience may end up providing more insight for some people than the preceding chapters.

Parents have difficulty in coping with a child who has declared his (or her) intention to live as a woman (or a man) and, possibly, seek reassignment surgery. Some may never adjust. Adjustment though varies among parents, which, arguably, is another way of saying it is a process. Different factors appear to affect this process, not the least of which is the sex of the parent. I have often wondered, in the case of male to female transsexuals, whether, contrary to conventional wisdom, adjustment is more straightforward for fathers. What if my other daughter instead had made the announcement that she wanted to live as a man and was contemplating reassignment surgery? Although this question is hypothetical, I am not so sure I would have responded the same way I responded to my more recent daughter's declaration nearly a decade ago. Of course, alternatively, it may be the case that the sex of the parent in relation to a child is really unimportant. What could be the critical factor is the nature of the relationship they have, with a sound bond being the determinant of a parent's capacity to adjust to having a daughter instead of a son, or vice versa.

It is easy for me now to see with the benefit of hindsight that it takes time to acknowledge what your child has just announced and reach a level of adjustment that even allows for harmonious everyday contact. Too often we overlook the importance of the role of the passage of time, especially concerning developments in personal relationships. Although there are those phrases that implicitly acknowledge that importance (for example, the value of 'biding for time'), their message is often muted when they differ: 'time heals all wounds' yet 'absence makes the heart grow fonder'! I think in my own case that, although there was conflict and tension at home for at least a year after my daughter announced her intentions, I am thankful I did not do anything in that early period to separate us. Time was important. It helped demonstrate the strength of my daughter's conviction and determination. This was no mere fad: it was real. I believe I had come a long way the day my daughter, in response to my predictable negative ranting about what she had planned, said that she would 'still be the same person'. What brought me to a halt though was her comment 'I am not going to die'. I felt guilty for having made her life difficult. I think I had begun to adjust to my new reality because I had reached the point where I could see that there were only two options and one was unacceptable. Either I accepted the situation or I would lose my daughter. Unfortunately, for many transsexuals, loss of family often results from parents not seeing the limited options they have. For me, seeing the options clearly, when I reflect on it, was a watershed because I moved from acknowledging the reality of what my daughter was about to do, to accepting her right and autonomy to do it. Later, I would encourage her to do it.

Adjustment is not merely a process but a two way process. Just as I (and my wife) no longer feel self-conscious about using 'she' and 'her' and our daughter's name, she in turn accepts that her parents have a history of having had a son and that cannot be altered. Those early years were very enjoyable, as are our memories of that period. Now we no longer have differences with our daughter over our wanting to keep old family photographs. This is one small indication that we have all come a long way together!

NOTES

1 At the time of writing this last chapter I received information of a new book on transsexualism through the Transgen network. Written by Gordene Olga Mackenzie, *Transgender Nation* (Bowling Green State University Press, 1994) describes itself on the back cover as follows:

> *Transgender Nation* dares to look at the male to woman transgenderist and transsexual from a sociocultural and sociopolitical perspective and maintains that it is not the individual transgenderist that is sick and in need of treatment but rather the culture that must be treated.

2 Foucault (1978: 87) claims that 'in western societies since the Middle Ages, the exercise of power has always been formulated in terms of law'. This is certainly true in the case of control of sexual relations, as evidenced by the emergence of laws governing who can marry, when they can marry and the nature of dissolution of marriage.

3 Contemporary transsexualism may, as Hausman (1992: 274n) suggests, represent 'a phenomenon distinct from earlier examples of cross-sex behaviors'. Notwithstanding her lack of evidence for this assertion, it may be the case that she confuses form with content. If her focus is on content, then the interplay of technology, agency and subjectivity clearly presents a different picture of transsexualism today. If, however, she regards contemporary transsexualism as the outward, adaptive manifestation of a psychosexual identity different from those cross sexed identities that, historically, sat uneasily beside the dichotomy of heterosexual men and women, then her argument is weak. Bullough (1975), whom she opposes, presents a good case for there being a long history of people with psychosexual identities unable to conform to a socially approved heterosexual man–woman dichotomy (see also Bullough 1976a; 1976b).

4 It has been suggested to me that homosexual couples have in the past been socially accepted as a legitimate family. Whether that was the case or not, at least over the past two or, possibly, three centuries there appears to be no evidence indicating that the family was anything other than the socially legitimate, heterosexual man–woman union.

5 Hausman, Millot and Collyer are just three scholars who see the post-operative transsexual as a product, in part, of current medical technology. Not all, however, make this point equally clearly. Note the following excerpt from Millot:

the transsexual, who is formed through assignation by the Other—a doctor or psychologist—finds an obdurate and even fallacious response to the enigma of his desire when he encounters his Other in Science. The desire of the Other is no longer veiled, the verdict is pronounced: let him be operated on. The Other desires his real castration. The discovery of a solution to the enigma of desire of the Other, such that one becomes its object, provokes a certain euphoria. But there is always a residue. Transsexuals are witness to this (1990: 142).

6 Whether politically involved or not, these transsexuals' conventional gender orientation may pose more of a problem than appears at face level. Hausman (1992: 302), for example, suggests that that orientation 'may serve as a cover for the destabilizing multiplicity of sexed positions made available through developments in medical technology'. Of course, 'may' is the key word and can only be accepted in the same sense as 'maybe–maybe not'.

7 See for the United Kingdom (Tully 1992: 7); the Netherlands (Snaith *et al.* 1993; Kuiper and Cohen-Kettenis 1988); the USA (Abramowitz 1986; Matto 1974: 207–208; Stuart 1983: 29, 123–124). See also Green (1992).

References

Abercrombie, N., Hill, S. and Turner, B. (1980) *The Dominant Ideology Thesis*, London: George Allen & Unwin.

Abramowitz, Stephen I. (1986) 'Psychosocial outcomes of sex re-assignment surgery', *Journal of Consulting and Clinical Psychology*, 54(2): 183-189.

Archer, John and Lloyd, Barbara (1987) *Sex and Gender*, Cambridge: Cambridge University Press.

Australia (1993) Australian Bureau of Statistics, Census Characteristics of Australia, cat. 2710.0: 17.

Bakker, A., van Kesteren, P.J., Gooren, L.J. and Bezemer, P.D. (1993) 'The prevalence of transsexualism in The Netherlands', *Acta Psychiatrica Scandinavica*, 87(4): 237-38.

Bell, Angela (1989) 'In sexual limbo', *Sydney Morning Herald*, 23 January: 23.

Benjamin, H. (1966) *The Transsexual Phenomenon*, New York: Julian Press.

Berger, Peter I. and Luckmann, Thomas (1967) *The Social Construction of Reality*, New York: Anchor Books.

Berthelot, J. M. (1991) 'Sociological discourse and the body' in Featherstone, M., Hepworth, M. and Turner, B. S. eds, *The Body, Social Process and Cultural Theory*: 390-404.

Billings, D.B. and Urban, T. (1982) 'The socio-medical construction of transsexualism: an interpretation and critique', *Social Problems*, 29(3): 266-282.

Blackwood, E. (1984) 'Sexuality and gender in certain native American tribes: the case of cross-gender females', *Signs: Journal of Women in Culture and Society*, 10(11): 27-42.

Bolin, Anne (1987a) 'Transsexualism and the limits of traditional analysis', *American Behavioral Scientist*, 31(1): 41-65.

Bolin, Anne (1987b) *In Search of Eve: Transsexual Rites of Passage*, South Hadley, Massachusetts: Bergin & Garvey.

Bower, Herbert (1986) 'Diagnosis and differential diagnosis: homosexual, transvestite or transsexual', in Walters and Ross eds, *Transsexualism and Sex Reassignment*: 44-51.

Brake, M. (1976) 'I may be queer but at least I am a man' in Barker, D. L. and Allen, S. eds, *Sexual Divisions and Society: Process and Change*, London: Tavistock.

Brown, George R. (1990) 'A review of the clinical approaches to gender dysphoria', *Journal of Clinical Psychiatry*, 51(2): 57-64.

Buchbinder, David (1994) *Masculinities and Identities*, Melbourne: Melbourne University Press.

Bullough, V. (1975) 'Transsexualism in history', *Archives of Sexual Behavior*, 4: 561-571.

Bullough, V. (1976a) *Sexual Variance in Society and History*, New York: John Wiley & Sons.

Bullough, V. (1976b) *Sex, Society and History*, New York: Science History Publications.

Burnard, Don and Ross, Michael W. (1986) 'Psychological aspects and psychological testing: what can psychological testing reveal?' in Walters and Ross eds, *Transsexualism and Sex Reassignment*: 52-63.

Callendar, C., and Kochems, L.M. (1983) 'The North American berdache', *Current Anthropology*, 24(4): 443-456.

Canary, C. (1974) *Canary: The Story of a Transsexual*, Los Angeles: Nash.

Collyer, F. (1994) 'Sex change surgery: an "unacceptable innovation?"' in *The Australian and New Zealand Journal of Sociology*, 30(1): 3-19.

Connell, R.W. (1983) *Which Way Is Up? Essays On Class, Sex and Culture*, Sydney: George Allen & Unwin.

Connell, R.W. (1987) *Gender and Power: Society, the Person and Sexual Politics*, Cambridge: Polity Press.

Cossey, Caroline (1991) *My Story*, London: Faber & Faber.

Cowell, R. (1954) *Roberta Cowell's Story By Herself*, London: Heinemann.

Crawford, Anne (1994) 'Woman trapped in a man's body finds solace', *The Sunday Age*, 3 July: 6.

Creed, G. (1984) 'Sexual subordination: institutionalised homosexuality and social control in Melanesia', *Ethnology*, 23: 156-176.

Cummings, Katherine (1992) *Katherine's Diary: The Story of a Transsexual*, Melbourne: Heinemann.

Daily Sun (1985) 'Ring-in Delores stuns glamor judges', 3 April: 1.

Davies, Bronwyn (1990) 'The problem of desire', *Social Problems*, 37(4): 501-516.

D'Emilio, J. (1983) 'Capitalism and gay identity' in Snitow, A., Stansell, C. and Thompson, S. eds, *Desire: The Politics of Sexuality*, London: Virago Press: 140-152.

Denny, Dallas (1994) *Gender Dysphoria: A Guide To Research*, New York: Garland.

Devor, Holly (1987) 'Gender blending females: women and sometimes men', *American Behavioral Scientist*, 31(1): 12-40.

Devor, Holly (1989) *Gender Blending: Confronting the Limits of Duality*, Bloomington: Indiana University Press.

Docter, Richard F. (1988) *Transvestites and Transsexuals: Towards a Theory of Cross Gender Behavior*, New York: Plenum Press.

Edelmann, Robert J. (1986) 'Adaptive training for existing male transsexual gender role: a case history', *The Journal of Sex Research*, 22(4): 514-519.

Eichler, M. (1980) *The Double Standard: A Feminist Critique of Feminist Social Science*, New York: St. Martin's Press.

Ekins, Richard (1993) 'On male femaling: a grounded theory approach to cross dressing and sex changing', *The Sociological Review*, 41(1): 1-29.

Eklund, P.L.E., Gooren, L.J.G. and Bezemer, P.D. (1988) 'The prevalence of transsexualism in The Netherlands', *British Journal of Psychiatry*, 152: 638-40.

Emerson, Joan (1970) 'Behavior in private places: sustaining definitions of reality in gynaecological examinations' in Dreitzel, H. ed., *Recent Sociology No 2*, London: Macmillan.

Falkiner, Suzanne (1988) *Eugenia: A Man*, Sydney and London: Pan Books.

Fallowell, Duncan and Ashley, April (1982) *April Ashley's Odyssey*, London: Jonathon Cape.

Featherstone, M., Hepworth, M. and Turner, B. S. eds. (1991) *The Body, Social Process and Cultural Theory*, London: Sage.

Feinbloom, D.H. (1976) *Transvestites and Transsexuals: Mixed Views*, New York: Delcorte/Seymour Lawrence.

Finlay, H.A. (1988) 'The legal position of transsexuals' in Finlay, H.A. and Walters, William A.W. (1988) *Sex Change: Medical and Legal Aspects of Sex Reassignment*: 43-137.

Finlay, H.A. and Walters, William A.W. (1988) *Sex Change: Medical and Legal Aspects of Sex Reassignment*, Box Hill, Victoria: H.A. Finlay.

Fleming, M.Z., MacGowan, B.R., Robinson, L., Spitz, J. and Salt, P. (1982) 'The body image of the post-operative female to male transsexual', *Journal of Consulting and Clinical Psychology*, 50: 461-462.

Forgey, D.G. (1975) 'The institution of the berdache among the North American plains indians', *Journal of Sex Research*, 11(1): 1-15.

Foucault, Michel (1978) *The History of Sexuality*, vol. 1. New York: Pantheon Books.

Foucault, Michel (1980) *Herculine Barbin*, Brighton, Sussex: The Harvester Press.

Frank, Arthur W. (1990) 'Bringing bodies back in: a decade review', *Theory, Culture and Society*, 7: 131-162.

Freimuth, Marilyn J. and Hornstein, Gail A. (1982) 'A critical examination of the concept of gender', *Sex Roles*, 8(5): 515-532.

Fry, J. (1974) *The Autobiography of Jane Fry*, New York: Wiley.

Fulton, R. and Anderson, S.W. (1992) 'The Amerindian "man–woman": gender liminality and cultural continuity', *Current Anthropology*, 33(5): 603-609.

Garber, Marjorie (1993) *Vested Interests: Cross Dressing and Cultural Anxiety*, Harmondsworth, Middlesex: Penguin.

Garfinkel, Harold and Stoller, Robert J. (1967) 'Passing and the managed achievement of sex status in an "intersexed" person part 1' in Garfinkel, Harold ed., *Studies in Ethnomethodology*, Englewood Cliffs, NJ: Prentice Hall: 116-185; 285-288.

Gatens, Moira (1983) 'A critique of the sex/gender distinction' in Allen, J. and Patten, P. eds., *Beyond Marxism? Interventions After Marx*, Sydney: Intervention Publications: 143-160.

Gender and Society (1992) 6(2).

Giddens, Anthony (1991) *Modernity and Self-Identity: Self and Society in the Late Modern Age*, Stanford, California: Stanford University Press.

Goh, Victor H.H. (1991) 'Transsexualism: a crisis in gender identity in males and females' in Ratnam, S.S., Goh, Victor H.H. and Tsoi, W.F. eds., *Cries From Within: Transsexualism, Gender Confusion and Sex Change*: 1-24.

Goodman, Raymond E. (1983) 'Biology and sexuality: inborn determinants of human sexual response', *British Journal of Psychiatry*, 143: 216-220.

Gough, Kathleen (1975) 'The origins of the family' in Reiter, Rayna R. ed., *Toward An Anthropology of Women*, New York and London: Monthly Review Press: 51-76.

Grant, J. (1983) *George and Julia*, London: Pan Books.

Green, R. (1969) 'Mythological, historical and cross cultural aspects of transsexualism' in Green, R. and Money, J. eds, *Transsexualism and Sex Reassignment*: 13-22.

Green, Richard (1974) *Sexual Identity Conflict in Children and Adults*, Baltimore, Md: Penguin Books Inc.

Green, Richard (1992) *Sexual Science and the Law*, Cambridge, Mass: Harvard University Press.

Green, Richard and Fleming, Davis T. (1990) 'Transsexual surgery follow up: status in the 1990s', *Annual Review of Sex Research*, 1: 163–174.

Green, Richard and Money, John eds (1969) *Transsexualism and Sex Reassignment*, Baltimore: Johns Hopkins University Press.

Greenberg, D.F. (1985) 'Why was the berdache ridiculed?', *Journal of Homosexuality*, 11(4): 179–189.

Greer, Germaine (1986) 'Review of *Conundrum* by Jan Morris' in her *The Mad Woman's Underclothes: Essays and Occasional Writings 1968–1985*, London: Picador: 189–191.

Greer, Germaine (1989) 'Once a man, always a man', *The Age*, 13 September.

Grimm, David E. (1987) 'Toward a theory of gender: transsexualism, gender, sexuality and relationships', *American Behavioral Scientist*, 31(1): 66–85.

Halperin, David M. (1990) *One Hundred Years of Homosexuality and Other Essays on Greek Love*, New York and London: Routledge.

Harding, Sue (1986) 'Welfare services for transsexuals: non-medical assistance' in Walters and Ross eds, *Transsexualism and Sex Reassignment*: 114–125.

Harvey, Sandra (1994) 'Transsexuals dying from loneliness, survey finds', *Sydney Morning Herald*, 13 April: 8.

Hausman, Bernice L. (1992) 'Demanding subjectivity: transsexualism, medicine, and the technologies of gender', *Journal of the History of Sexuality*, 3(2): 270–302.

Herdt, G. (1989) 'Father presence and ritual homosexuality: paternal deprivation and masculine development in Melanesia reconsidered', *Ethos*, 17(3): 326–370.

Herdt, Gilbert (1990) 'Mistaken gender: 5-alpha reductase hermaphroditism and biological reductionism in sexual identity reconsidered', *American Anthropologist*, 92(2): 433–446.

Hirschman, Albert O. (1970) *Exit, Voice and Loyalty*, Cambridge, Massachusetts: Harvard University Press.

Hodgkinson, Liz (1987) *Bodyshock: The Truth About Changing Sex*, London: Columbus Books.

Imperato-McGinley, J., Peterson, R.E., Gautier, T. and Sturla, E. (1979) 'Androgens and the evolution of male gender identity among male pseudohermaphrodites with 5 alpha reductase deficiency', *New England Journal of Medicine*, 300: 1233–37.

Jackson, Peter (1989) *Maps of Meaning*, London: Unwin Hyman.

Johnson, Chris and Brown, Cathy with Nelson, Wendy (1982) *The Gender Trap*, London & New York: Proteus.

Jorgenson, Christine (1968) *Christine Jorgenson: A Personal Autobiography*, New York: Bantam Books.

Kando, T. (1973) *Sex Change*, Springfield, Illinois: Charles C. Thomas.

Kessler, Suzanne (1990) 'The medical construction of gender: case management of intersexed infants', *Signs: Journal of Women in Culture and Society*, 16(1): 3-24.

Kessler, Suzanne J. and McKenna, Wendy (1985) *Gender: An Ethnomethodological Approach*, New York: John Wiley.

King, Dave (1981) 'Gender confusions: psychological and psychiatric conceptions of transvestism and transsexualism' in Plummer, Kenneth ed., *The Making of the Modern Homosexual*, London: Hutchinson: 155-183.

King, D. (1984) 'Condition, orientation, role or false conciousness? Models of homosexuality and transsexualism', *Sociological Review*, 32(1): 38-56.

King, Dave (1993) *The Transvestite and the Transsexual: Public Categories and Private Identities*, Aldershot: Avebury.

Kirby, M.D. (1988) 'Foreword' in Finlay, H.A. and Walters, William A.W., *Sex Change: Medical and Legal Aspects of Sex Reassignment*, Box Hill, Victoria: H.A. Finlay: v-ix.

Kubler-Ross, Elizabeth (1970) *On Death and Dying*, London: Tavistock Publications.

Kuiper, B. and Cohen-Kettenis, P. (1988) 'Sex reassignment surgery: a study of 141 Dutch transsexuals', *Archives of Sexual Behaviour*, 17: 439-457.

Lancet (1991) Editorial 'Transsexualism', vol. 338, September: 603-604.

Laub, Donald R. and Gandy, Patrick eds, (1973) *Proceedings of the Second Interdisciplinary Symposium on Gender Dysphoria Syndrome*, Stanford: Stanford University Medical Centre.

Leo, John (1985) 'Battling over masochism', *Time*, 2 December: 68.

Lewins, Frank (1992a) *Social Science Methodology: A Brief But Critical Introduction*, Melbourne: Macmillan Education Australia.

Lewins, Frank (1992b) 'Everyday culture in China: the experience of Chinese intellectuals' in *China Information*, 7(2): 56-69.

Lindenbaum, S. (1984) 'Variations on a sociosexual theme in Melanesia' in Herdt, G. ed., *Ritualised Homosexuality in Melanesia*, London: University of California Press.

Lindgren, T.W. and Pauly, I.B. (1975) 'A body image scale for evaluating transsexuals', *Archives of Sexual Behaviour*, 4: 639-656.

Lopez, Elisabeth (1991) 'The other woman was her husband', *The Age*, 5 June: 18.

Matto, Michele (1974) 'The transsexual in society' in Truzzi, Marcello ed., *Sociology For Pleasure*, Englewood Cliffs, NJ: Prentice Hall: 192-209.

Middleton, Karen (1993) 'A father's love for his child that transcends the sex boundaries', *The Age*, 30 October: 3.

Millot, Catherine (1990) *Horesexe: Essay On Transsexuality*, translated by Kenneth Hylton, New York: Autonomedia Inc.

Money, John (1968) *Sex Errors of the Body*, Baltimore: Johns Hopkins University Press.

Money, John (1976) 'Gender identity and hermaphroditism: letter', *Science*, 191: 872.

Money, John (1988) *Gay, Straight and In-Between: The Sexology of Erotic Orientation*, New York: Oxford University Press.

Money, John and Ehrhardt, A. (1972) *Man & Woman Boy & Girl: The Differentiation and Dimorphism of Gender Identity from Conception to Maturity*, Baltimore: Johns Hopkins University Press.

Money, John and Tucker, Patricia (1977) *Sexual Signatures: On Being A Man Or A Woman*, London: Abacus.

Mostyn, Suzanne (1993) 'Gender seen in perspective', *Sydney Morning Herald*, 27 November: 11.

Morris, Jan (1987) *Conundrum*, Harmondsworth: Penguin Books.

New Idea (1989) 'Tragedy of the mum who became a man', 22 April: 12-13.

New Woman (1993) 'Women who want to be men', March: 46-49.

Perkins, Roberta (1983) *The 'Drag Queen' Scene: Transsexuals in Kings Cross*, Sydney: George Allen & Unwin.

Perkins, Roberta, Griffin, Aidy and Jakobsen, Jeddah (1994) *Transgender Lifestyles and HIV/AIDS Risk*, Canberra: Australian Government Publishing Service.

Pringle, Rosemary (1992) 'Absolute sex? Unpacking the sexuality/gender relationship' in Connell, R. W. and Dowsett, G. W. eds, *Rethinking Sex: Social Theory and Sexuality Research*, Melbourne: Melbourne University Press: 76-101.

Ratnam, S.S., Goh, Victor H.H., Anandakumar, C. and Tham, K.F. (1991) 'Sex change surgery' in Ratnam, S.S., Goh, Victor H.H. and Tsoi, W.F. eds, *Cries From Within: Transsexualism, Gender Confusion and Sex Change*: 57-76.

Ratnam, S.S., Goh, Victor H.H. and Tsoi, W.F. eds, (1991) *Cries From Within: Transsexualism, Gender Confusion and Sex Change*, Singapore: Longman.

Raymond, Janice G. (1979) *The Transsexual Empire*, Boston: Beacon Press.

Richards, Renee with John Ames (1983) *Second Serve: The Renee Richards Story*, New York: Stein & Day.

Riseley, Donna (1986) 'Gender identity disorder of childhood: diagnostic and treatment issues' in Walters and Ross eds, *Transsexualism and Sex Reassignment*: 26–43.

Ross, Michael W. (1986a) 'Gender identity: male, female or third gender' in Walters and Ross eds, *Transsexualism and Sex Reassignment*: 1–8.

Ross, Michael W. (1986b) 'Causes of gender dysphoria : how does transsexualism develop and why?' in Walters and Ross eds, *Transsexualism and Sex Reassignment*: 16–25.

Rubin, G. (1975) 'The traffic in women: notes on the "political economy" of sex' in Reiter, R. R. ed., *Toward An Anthropology of Women*, New York: Monthly Review Press: 157–210.

Sagarin, E. (1978) 'Transsexualism: legitimation, amplification and exploitation of deviance by scientists and mass media' in Winick, C. ed., *Deviance and Mass Media*, Beverly Hills: Sage.

Sinclair, Abby (1965) *I Was Male*, Chicago: Novel Books.

Singer, June (1977) *Androgyny: Towards a New Theory of Sexuality*, London: Routledge & Kegan Paul.

Snaith, P., Tarsh, M.J. and Reid, R. (1993) 'Sex reassignment surgery: a study of 141 Dutch transsexuals', *British Journal of Psychiatry*, 162: 681–85.

Steinbeck, A. W. (1986) 'Endocrine aspects: hormones and their role' in Walters and Ross eds, *Transsexualism and Sex Reassignment*: 64–81.

Stirling, Peter (1989) *So Different*, Brookvale, NSW: Simon and Schuster.

Stoller, R. (1968) *Sex and Gender: On the Development of Masculinity and Femininity*, New York: Science House.

Stuart, Kim Elizabeth (1983) *The Uninvited Dilemma*, Lake Oswego, Oregon: Metamorphous Press.

Synnott, Anthony (1989) 'Shame and glory: a sociology of hair', *British Journal of Sociology*, 38(3): 381–413.

Synnott, Anthony (1993) *The Body Social: Symbolism, Self and Society*, London: Routledge.

Thayer, J.S. (1980) 'The berdache of the northern plains: a socioreligious perspective', *Journal of Anthropological Research*, 36(3): 287–293.

Townsend, Helen (1978) 'Transexual: a life of living a lie', *Forum*, 6(8): 26–32.

Truth (1990) 'Sex-changer ditched by her dream lover', 6 January.

Tsoi, W.F. (1991) 'Psychological profiles of transsexuals' in Ratnam, S.S., Goh, Victor H.H. and Tsoi, W.F. eds, *Cries From Within:*

Transsexualism, Gender Confusion and Sex Change: 31–46.

Tully, Bryan (1992) *Accounting For Transsexualism and Transhomosexuality*, London: Whiting & Birch Ltd.

Turner, B. S. (1984) *The Body and Society: Explorations in Social Theory*, Oxford: Basil Blackwell.

Turner, B. S. (1991) 'Recent developments in the theory of the body' in Featherstone, M., Hepworth, M. and Turner, B. S. eds, *The Body, Social Process and Cultural Theory*: 1–35.

Turner, B. S. (1992) *Regulating Bodies: Essays in Medical Sociology*, London: Routledge.

Walters, William A.W. (1986) 'Ethical aspects: is gender reassignment morally acceptable?' in Walters and Ross eds, *Transsexualism and Sex Reassignment*: 126–134.

Walters, William (1988) 'Human sexual differentiation and its disturbances' in Finlay and Walters *Sex Change: Medical and Legal Aspects of Sex Reassignment*: 1–42.

Walters, William A.W., Kennedy, Trudy and Ross, Michael W. (1986) 'Results of gender reassignment: is it all worthwhile?' in Walters and Ross eds, *Transsexualism and Sex Reassignment:* 144–151.

Walters, William A.W. and Ross, Michael W. eds. (1986) *Transsexualism and Sex Reassignment*, Melbourne: Oxford University Press.

Wells, Elizabeth (1986) 'The view from within: what it feels like to be a transsexual' in Walters and Ross eds, *Transsexualism and Sex Reassignment*: 9–15.

Whitam, F.L. (1987) 'A cross-cultural perspective on homosexuality, transvestism and transsexualism' in Wilson, G.D., *Variant Sexuality: Research and Theory*, Kent: Croom Helm Ltd.

Wikan, U. (1977) 'Man becomes woman: transsexualism in Oman as a key to gender roles', *Man*, 12: 304–319.

Williams, W. L. (1985) 'Persistence and change in the berdache tradition among contemporary Lakota Indians', *Journal of Homosexuality*, 11(4): 191–200.

Williams, Walter L. (1987) 'Women, men and others', *American Behavioral Scientist*, 31(1): 135–141.

Woman's Day (1988) 'The trauma of being a transsexual', 26 April: 25–27.

Woman's Day (1989) 'Goodbye Alan, hello Helen ... and happiness', 19 December: 12–13.

Woman's Day (1993) 'My son is now my daughter', 22 November: 36–37.

Woodhouse, Annie (1989) *Fantastic Women: Sex, Gender and Transvestism*, London: Macmillan.

Index